TELEVISION STATION MANAGEMENT

The Business of Broadcasting

Television Station Management

The Business of Broadcasting

Edited by Yale Roe

Contributors

GEORGE A. BAKER • JULIUS BARNATHAN

HOWARD W. COLEMAN • VERNON F. COOK • JAY CROUSE

MILTON D. FRIEDLAND • ALBERT JOHN GILLEN

COLBY LEWIS • JAMES K. MIKITA • RICHARD B. RAWLS

LAWRENCE H. ROGERS II • JOHN B. SIAS

SIDNEY V. STADIG • EDWARD A. WARREN

EDWARD WETTER • CHARLES YOUNG • NORMAN ZIEGLER

Communication Arts Books

HASTINGS HOUSE, PUBLISHERS

New York 22

CONTENTS

PREFACE

TELEVISION broadcasting is certainly one of the most exciting and exhilarating businesses in today's society. There is a kinetic quality that one feels, a sense of exuberance that comes from being so vitally involved in the drama of life. For television is a business of ideas and communication, and inherent in its very being is one of the most basic elements of human existence, the interaction of man's thoughts. Throughout this panorama of activity are woven the threads of mankind's interests. For the scientist there is the challenge of man talking to man and looking at man, across continents and oceans and through a medium that is part of space. For the educator there is the thrill of learning from the source material of life as Arnold Toynbee discusses history, Harry Truman speaks on the presidency, Judith Anderson recreates Medea, or the New York Philharmonic projects the heroic music of Beethoven. For the businessman there is the movement of merchandise, the sale of goods, the economic activity that builds and sustains the broad middle class that, as Aristotle long ago observed, is requisite to the stability of a democracy. For the viewer there are people whom he never would have met, cities he never would have visited, events he never would have witnessed, entertainment he never would have enjoyed. And so, in a sense, television presents the broad sweep of life and, like life, has moments of nobility and others of excess. It is all of this, this total involvement in life, that makes the television business a fascinating experience.

Nonetheless, life cannot be and is not lived in a state of constant euphoria. Rather it is the sum of many separate duties that result in the final and complete act. It is the purpose of this book to examine those duties that together make up the business of broadcasting. This is an attempt to examine the realities of the business as reported by the men who live its daily challenges. The men who are represented here are among the outstanding broadcasters in the country. Each is unusually well qualified to discuss the specific facet of the business in which he is personally involved. Furthermore, these men together provide a broad picture of the television industry, for they represent commercial and educational stations, as well as those that are independent and network-affiliated. They also speak from every part of the country, from large and small television markets, and from virtually every station group in the country.

The men who have written these chapters earn their livings and support their families by doing the jobs they describe. The problems and the challenges they write about are the real ones. Not every broadcaster will agree with every attitude herein expressed. But disagreement will probably be only a matter of degree. For all broadcasters are faced with the same basic problems of television station management.

The functions of broadcasting aside, it is interesting to look at the broadcaster himself. Just who is the man behind this social revolution called television? The skeptic might see him as a manipulator of the public culture. A student might envision him as the new leader of public opinion. A wife may view him as the man who never is able to get home for dinner until after the children are asleep.

This man, the broadcaster, is not a person acting out sublimated psychoses by perpetrating violence over the public air waves. Nor is he a bold crusader for social causes which his own public does not support. The fact of the matter is that he is most likely a man with a good scholastic background, that he may well be a college graduate, that he is married, loves his children, worries about the bomb, works too hard, and either plays golf or wishes he did. He reads books, thinks thoughts, and wonders if he will ever get away from the continuous pressure. More frequently than not, he is a member of the managerial class rather than having any significant ownership in the broadcasting property for which he is responsible. He worries and works so as to increase the company's profits, only to find himself under renewed pressure the following year to help increase profits still more. He satisfies the majority of his viewing public with entertainment programs, and then is chastised by letter-writers and TV columnists for those very same programs. He puts on other programs of social importance, and finds that only a small segment of his audience is watching them.

The broadcasters who have written these chapters have examined this syndrome, have described and discussed the professional problems that they face, and have suggested solutions to some of these problems. They offer the knowledge of their experience to readers interested in learning about the business of broadcasting.

The final dimension of a broadcaster must be supplied by each individual himself, and that is the dimension he brings to broadcasting as the man that he is. It is on these personal values, of the broadcaster as a man, that many decisions will turn. The broadcaster will find himself faced with many considerations: Can my newscasts have more substance? Can my editorials be more significant? Can my entertainment programs be of better quality? Shall I pre-empt prime-time entertainment for a serious analysis of an issue vital to the welfare of my viewers? Shall I be satisfied with a profit that exceeds last year's figures, but is less than the maximum possible, so that I can use more funds for important services for my viewers?

These are but a few of the questions that begin to transcend professional acumen and move into the area of personal values. These are but a few of the questions that every broadcaster must answer, not only as a broadcaster but also as a man.

The broadcaster is no saint on earth dedicated to mankind's salvation through the uplifting force of television. Nor is he the devil incarnate seeking to wrest the last possible dollar from the last possible advertiser, indifferent to the social implications of his action. Rather he is more likely to be a somewhat lonely man, friendly with his employers and employees, and yet somewhat isolated from both, promulgating some programming with a twinge of conscience and other programming with a sense of pride—and yet perhaps not quite sure the former is so very bad or the latter so very significant. He has moments of courage and others of fear; moments of conviction and others of doubt. He is, in fact, simply another human being, very much like everyone else.

Except for one thing—he is the man with the responsibility.

YALE ROE

FOREWORD

TELEVISION has become the great "either-or" phenomenon of American society. It is either a saint or a sinner, either the direct path upward toward the fulfillment of individual man within a free society, or the primrose path downward to the subtle social hell of "mass man" in a consumer society. More to the point, however, is the simple dichotomy which underlies the others; television is either a public service, or it is a business. Actually the latter reference ought to be framed in a different way. TV is either a business, or it does not exist; and if it does not exist the question of whether profit and "public service" are compatible concepts is rhetorical.

Educators specializing in the fields of broadcasting and the mass media, therefore, were not long in discovering that tomorrow's decision-makers in TV must be brought into touch not only with those disciplines which treat television as a potential art form or as a wider socio-cultural phenomenon, but also with the crucial area of sound economic management. The need for direct and intensive training in the practical day-to-day problems of business in TV is vital to the education of future broadcasters, who must understand where the dollars come from and how they must be applied in providing a maximum television service. This capacity to understand and work with the laws of economic survival is, it should be added, as important to students who seek a career in non-commercial television as to those who will enter the commercial field. If anything, the laws of efficient economic operation apply even more stringently in ETV, where the supply of dollars is tighter and managerial inefficiency therefore less tolerable. At some point along the line, ETV operators, too, must recognize that public acceptance will inevitably determine operating budgets.

The concern of broadcast educators is reflected in the variety of formal courses now being offered which treat this important aspect of broadcasting. To date, however, there have been few, if any, practical texts in this field, and it is for this reason that Yale Roe has given us a volume of singular importance.

Mr. Roe is an experienced television executive with a sure sense of the way in which efficient television operation is conducted. He has invited a number of his colleagues from various specialized fields within television to contribute timely and practical observations about the specific problems of television management. The result is an anthology of forthright, from-the-shoulder descriptions of what works and what doesn't work in all phases of television's business operation.

This is the first text devoted entirely to management and operation of the television station, and it should rank among the best for a long time to come. There is little "theory" here, and therein lies the great virtue of the work—for teachers, for students, and for the perpetuation of a free and vital television in this land.

A. WM. BLUEM
Associate Professor:
S.I. Newhouse School of Communications
Syracuse University

PART ONE

THE BUSINESS OF BROADCASTING

CHAPTER 1

The Business
of Broadcasting

BY LAWRENCE H. ROGERS II

Taft Broadcasting Company, Cincinnati, Ohio

A native of New Jersey, Mr. Rogers had graduated from Princeton University, served as an Artillery Captain in World War II in Europe, and had become one of television's earliest pioneers by the time he was 27. After a decade as operator of one of the nation's first stations, during which time he was a founder and Board Chairman of the Television Bureau of Advertising, he joined Taft Broadcasting Company, Cincinnati, Ohio, of which he is now President.

PUBLIC broadcasting in the United States is a communications force unique in the history of mankind. Coupling the emission of electronic wireless signals through the atmosphere with the mass advertising techniques peculiar to the American free-enterprise economy, private industry, operating under technical ground rules promulgated by the federal government, has in the space of two generations connected virtually every American household into a visual and aural communications network operating around the clock.

There is practically no populated area of the United States outside the coverage of a radio or television signal of usable proportions. There is no significant portion of the American population which is not continually in contact with radio and television broadcasts. Radio and television receiving apparatus outnumber in total and in penetration all the commonly accepted household appliances of the day, including such "necessities" as telephones, refrigeration, and even indoor plumbing.

All forms of broadcasting utilize basically similar techniques for long-distance transmission of electronic signals, generically referred to as "radio"; although the different techniques are usually grouped in popular categories: AM, FM, and TV.

AM BROADCASTING

Let us begin with so-called "AM Radio," the first segment of the industry to be developed, and the service with the widest distribution both in home receivers and in broadcasting transmitters.

"AM" is the abbreviation for amplitude modulation, and as the name implies, it is a technique for recreating sounds by variations in the transmission power. It is roughly comparable to the physical activation of the vocal chords, or the transmitter diaphragm of a telephone, with the additional factor of wireless transmission.

The growth of AM broadcasting was rather deliberate from its beginnings. It received its most important impetus from the introduction by the Radio Corporation of America of the so-called "music box"; a radio receiver capable of reproducing sounds of the human voice and music, rather than the continuous wave "dot-dash" broadcasting that had preceded it. Under the direction of David Sarnoff, RCA conceived the notion of providing entertainment programs, mostly music, in order to spur its development and sale of these "music boxes." This led to the connection of several transmitting stations by telephone wires in order to pool the production and expense of programs. This was the beginning of the NBC network, and the real beginning of broadcasting as a viable commercial entity.

By the time of World War II, the AM broadcasting art had reached a high state of development, with about 900 stations serving most of the United States, and with four competing radio networks: the Columbia Broadcasting System; the Mutual Broadcasting System; and the Red and Blue Networks of the National Broadcasting Company. This was the so-called "golden age of radio" during which the highly popular nighttime features such as *Amos 'n' Andy, Jack Benny, Information Please, Bob Hope, Bing Crosby,* and dozens of others reached national audiences rivaling those of the more popular television programs of today. It is noteworthy that this entire development was made on the basis of advertising support of programs on the national and the local level.

There was never any serious effort to underwrite the cost of the development of radio through subscription, tax support, or other means. It is also important that most radio program material was owned or controlled by the advertisers who paid for the time.

Radio as a responsible, and indispensable, medium of immediate news and current events commentary reached its highest state of development as a result of the events leading up to and during the Second World War.

REGULATORY HISTORY

The regulatory background of the development of AM radio provides a frame of reference against which to examine the later developments in broadcasting.

When it first arrived on the scene, commercial broadcasting, harking back to descriptions of the Dempsey-Firpo Heavyweight Fight, or the Harding Inauguration, was unregulated. It became immediately apparent, however, that something of a natural resource was involved in the use of the atmosphere for transmission. It was equally apparent that unrestricted transmission resulted in chaos. Therefore, the issuance of licenses to operate radio equipment was delegated to the Department of Commerce, under then Secretary Herbert Hoover. By 1927 it was deemed necessary to formalize the parceling out of radio frequencies on a less haphazard basis, in order to protect existing licensees from undue interference, and to provide for a more orderly growth in the future. Accordingly the Federal Radio Act of 1927 was passed, establishing the Federal Radio Commission. This beginning was reorganized by the Communications Act of 1934 under which the existing regulatory bureau, the Federal Communications Commission, was activated as an administrative arm of Congress. The Communications Act of 1934, as amended, is still the "law of the land" under which all licensees are permitted to operate "in the public interest, convenience, and necessity."

In order to understand the need for this kind of regulation, it is only necessary to understand that the radio spectrum—that is the list of radio frequencies available to be utilized for transmission —is not unlimited. On the other hand, the number of uses to which electromagnetic energy can be put seems, in light of historical fact, to be limitless. Every time a radio signal is put into the air it uses a space in the transmission frequency that cannot be used for something else without some form of interference. Thus, the prime function of the FCC was originally as a technical traffic cop to insure that all the radio stations do not interfere with one another to such a point that none of them can be heard.

In the developmental days of AM, one only had to conduct a "frequency search" to determine that a certain frequency could be utilized without violating the rigid rules on interference that had been set up under the Acts of 1927 and 1934, to be granted use of that frequency. Later, the FCC accumulated in its body of Rules and Regulations the additional requirements of financial responsibility, ability and proven desire to serve the public, etc. This rather haphazard system resulted in the development of a nationwide advertising-supported radio industry at the end of World War II numbering some 930 AM facilities from coast to coast.

The technical, economic, and population upheavals of the World War II years brought forth an enormous boom in radio. Hundreds, indeed thousands, of would-be operators, attracted by the tales of limitless profits engendered by pre-war radio stations, flocked to the FCC. The FCC, responding to pressures from Congress, the White House, and the public at large, revised continually its rules and regulations regarding acceptable interference levels, and began pell mell to authorize new AM stations. This burgeoning growth in AM broadcasting, reaching down to the smallest communities in the nation, has resulted in some 3,800 AM radio stations in the land today.

Indeed, the overpopulation of some radio markets has become such an economic concern of the industry and the Commission that the FCC recently announced a "freeze" on new construction grants until some more sensible solution of the dilemma might be found.

FM BROADCASTING

While amplitude modulation, or AM, became the "standard broadcast" technique for American radio, it was not necessarily the only, or the best, form of the art. Various pioneers developed a parallel system of recreating sounds called "frequency modulation," or FM. The occupation of the radio spectrum by the various other forms of broadcasting that had "growed," like Topsy, forced the

FCC to assign some frequencies to the development and use of FM during the 30's. FM differs from AM, as the name would indicate, in the manner in which recreatable sound signals are transmitted through the ether: namely, by the variation of the frequency of transmission rather than the intensity of transmission. Whether because of the nature of the system, or because of the accident of its having been assigned much higher frequencies for use, FM claims as its principal advantage over AM a certain immunity to man-made interference. There was no significant development of FM as a commercial entity until after World War II.

At the same time as the issuance of hundreds of new AM permits in 1946, the FCC opened up a new band of FM station assignments. These were much heralded as the "new" and "superior" radio medium, perhaps with some justification. But, by and large, the FM assignments were taken on by existing AM operators, who proceeded to duplicate their AM programming on the new FM channels. A relatively few hardy souls tried separate FM programming, many of them attempting to recruit audiences with "good music" or predominantly classical repertoires. But there were few FM receivers in the hands of the public, and the absence of any significant new programming source precluded any large scale purchase of "tuners" or "converters" designed to enable AM receivers to pick up FM as well.

It is interesting to note, at this point, that the predecessor corporation of Taft Broadcasting Company, Radio Cincinnati, developed one of the most ambitious FM projects. This was known as "Transit Radio," and for a time was a national venture with affiliate stations in 22 major cities beaming FM music and shoppers' news commercials to special receivers in the local buses and streetcars. Born amid high hopes and great fanfare, this project died along with many other hopeful FM innovations.

Nevertheless, many broadcasting companies held on to their FM licenses, and a few, Radio Cincinnati among them, continued despite no source of income to counterprogram the AM medium with FM broadcasts in the classical music vein.

By the late 1950's nearly 4,000 AM stations crowded the air waves, and had managed to weather the onslaught of competition from television. But a major change had overcome radio, and the basic radio formula was hometown news and popular music, with the bizarre noise of "rhythm and blues," "hillbilly," and "rock 'n' roll" definitely in the ascendancy. Against this competitive background, the more selective radio audiences began to discover a treasure trove of light and classical music on FM, largely uninterrupted by commercial messages. In the very large metropolitan centers, FM broadcasting began to come into its own as a separately programmed advertising-supported music medium. The absence of interference and the extremely high fidelity of its reproduction made it ideal for a music-lover's medium. The development of high-fidelity tape recording and automatic devices made it possible to operate an FM franchise at very small cost.

Accordingly, today the FM broadcasting medium is gradually coming into its own, even to the extent of some of the overpopulation problems that have long plagued AM. Special purpose broadcasting, including sterephonic music, has become a popular FM tool.

Television Broadcasting

By far the most spectacular development in broadcasting is television. Television is, after all, merely an extension of radio transmission into visual as well as aural reproduction.

In fact, the confusing terminology of the industry ignores the fact that television's picture signal is an AM signal, and its sound signal is an FM signal. By this relatively simple means, both can be transmitted over the same range of frequencies at the same time without mutual interference. Notwithstanding this fact, we still refer to the three main forms as AM, FM, and TV.

Workable experiments in television transmission date from the late 20's, and substantially the system now in use in the U.S. was ready for launching by 1940. However, the commercial development was held up by the war.

In 1946 the FCC, at the same time it was issuing vast numbers of new AM and FM permits, announced the new standards for television licensing. Many recognized authorities in the broadcasting field—notably Eugene MacDonald, president of Zenith—voiced strong doubt that advertising dollar support in quantities huge enough to support the staggering costs involved in television would ever be feasible. Consequently, there was a vigorous movement to release television channels only on a subscription or "pay-as-you-see" basis.

The cost of erecting a television station in the late 40's was perhaps ten times, at a minimum, the cost of a community radio station. The operating costs seemed prohibitive; they were unknown, and there was little, if any, source of revenues. Advertising income was dependent upon receiver circulation, receiver circulation was dependent upon programming, which in turn required advertising "seed money." The same old "chicken and egg" cycle that nearly killed FM was facing television.

Most early television stations were erected on speculation by AM broadcasters, who depended upon their radio profits to keep alive their television step-children.

Significantly, NBC, the subsidiary broadcasting arm of RCA, supplied the primary impetus. NBC urged its affiliated radio stations to grab off TV franchises when they were available for the asking; and the network plowed millions into programming and facilities to feed programs to stations. Rather reluctantly and belatedly, CBS joined the parade. ABC, newly divorced from NBC by a Justice Department consent decree, saw an opportunity to emerge with a third competitive broadcasting service. So it jumped in early in an effort to head off CBS and cut down NBC's competitive advantage.

By late 1948, 108 TV stations had been authorized and at least partially constructed. Then the FCC discovered a rather startling error.

In setting up its standards, it had been assumed, as was the case in FM, that television signals could only reach on a "line of sight" path to the horizon. Accordingly, stations on the same frequencies could be placed much closer together than in AM. The basic reason for this phenomenon was that TV, like FM, is a much higher frequency system than AM. Indeed the channels reserved for television and FM broadcasting were both allocated in the so-called "Very High Frequency" spectrum, or roughly from 60 to 200 megacycles. AM, or the "standard broadcast band," is located between 500 and 1,600 kilocycles. By comparison this is the same as .5 to 1.6 megacycles, or conversely the same as saying that Channel 3 television is at 60,000 kilocycles.

At any event, this "Very High Frequency," or VHF television did not react in actuality the way it had on the drawing boards. Indeed it went around corners, over mountains, and through buildings in a most perplexing manner. This is especially true at the lower end of the TV band from 50 to 88 megacycles. Channels 2, 3, 4, 5, and 6 reached out much further, and covered difficult valley locations far better than had been anticipated. The "high" side of VHF, Channels 7 through 13, 174 to 216 megacycles, reacted much more as they had been predicted: namely, the higher the channel the more likely it would suffer "shadows" from obstructions and reach only to the horizon.

The net effect of early experience showed that if TV had been allowed to continue under the same standards, there would have been chaos. Stations would have interfered with each other to an even more disastrous extent than in AM. So on October 1, 1948, the FCC announced the now famous "TV Freeze."

For four and a half years, while FCC engineers promulgated new rules for television, no new facilities were allowed. During this period, with a government protected semi-monopoly, 108 stations and three networks brought television techniques and programming to an extremely high state of development and public acceptance. The majority of the nation was covered, and most of the program forms were developed. The myth of no advertising support was forever blasted; and TV took over the national advertising marketplace to a degree that has never since been dented.

In April, 1952, the FCC announced the end of the television "freeze" in the now classic "Sixth Report and Order."

In substance, the Sixth Report abolished, without benefit of new legislation, the old "catch as catch can" method of installing television and radio channels, and it established what is known as the "Table of Allocations." This is to say that the FCC designated, by mutually protected 180-mile-diameter circles on the map of the United States, the total extent to which the 12 VHF channels could be utilized to provide a nationwide competitive television service. The allocations were graduated by centers of population and economic growth. By way of example, seven VHF assignments each were allocated to New York and to Los Angeles; four each to Chicago and Washington; and one each to hundreds of smaller communities throughout the nation.

Incidentally, the FCC also took note of the disparity in performance between the "low band" VHF (Channels 2-6) and the "high band" (7-13) noted earlier. Because of spectrum crowding, the entire FM broadcasting band, strange as it seems, is located in the radio spectrum between Channel 6 television and Channel 7. In fact there is an enormous gap of 86 megacycles. This explains the differing characteristics of the low channel numbers and the high. Accordingly the FCC developed and included in the Sixth Report a formula by which this differential would be theoretically eliminated. The ratio is 1:3.16. That is to say, stations on the lower five VHF channels may operate with a maximum radiated power of 100 kilowatts (100,000 watts e.r.p.), while those seven in the high band can have a maximum of 316 kilowatts (316,000 watts, e.r.p.). As in most radio theory, it does not always work in practice. In flat, level terrain, a high numbered channel at 316 kw. can do as well as a low band at 100 kw. But in rough, mountainous terrain, the low band VHF channels have a tremendous advantage in coverage over high band assignments, regardless of power differential.

This is one of many technical phenomena that eventually reach their solutions in the marketplace. Nevertheless, the FCC has continually become more and more preoccupied with developing a "utopian" scheme of technical rules that would eliminate these differences. Such a utopia is, in the opinion of the writer, utterly impossible.

In light of predicted population growth and other factors, this allocation was hardly adequate to supply future demand for TV channels and to maintain a nationwide competitive balance of facilities.

As a result, a whole new spectrum of television broadcasting was opened up in the "Ultra High Frequency" band, or UHF. Previously these UHF channels, and even higher ones known as the "Microwaves," had been used only for point-to-point transmission.

Because of the extremely high frequency of the carrier waves, signals at these frequencies actually do operate much as light waves. For practical purposes they will not bend around the horizon, behind mountains, through high buildings, or even in some circumstances through heavy foliage.

Nevertheless, 69 new TV channels, numbered from 14 through 83, were opened up for commercial use in the UHF, presaging perhaps a couple of thousand new future TV stations.

The opening of the UHF band, unfortunately, was described by the then Chairman of the FCC, as the communications equivalent of the opening of the Oklahoma territory. In a prepared speech announcing the Sixth Report, he urged operators who had witnessed the growing power of TV during the freeze, and the sometimes monumental profits of pre-freeze VHF stations, to "stake out a claim" in this last new frontier of broadcasting.

To their sorrow, hundreds did. Many went broke. Many hung on during lean years until the FCC bailed them out with a new VHF assignment. A few score hardy souls hung on, and today there are a hundred UHF television stations on the air, with the prospect of hundreds more when the incubating period for successful small-town operation has been completed.

The FCC has repeatedly attempted to shift all assignments to UHF in order to eliminate the competitive and economic disparity between the VHF medium and the UHF. But technically it can be demonstrated that the net result would be a permanent loss of TV service to a substantial part of the nation. In addition, billions invested by the public in VHF apparatus would be lost forever. The Eighty-Seventh Congress called a halt to these proposals by directing the Commission to proceed with the further development of UHF without destroying the VHF service essential to a nationwide competitive TV system.

As a part of the truce in the VHF vs. UHF battle decreed by Congress, a new law was adopted requiring manufacturers to build TV receivers according to FCC standards that would include reception capabilities for all assigned broadcast frequencies: i.e., both the UHF Channels and the VHF Channels.

These so-called "all-channel receivers" began coming off the assembly lines during 1963 with a deadline under the law of April 1964. The results, it is hoped, will be that in due time all U.S. receivers will be capable of picking up signals of UHF channels as well as the entrenched VHF's. It is expected that this will eventually lead to the acceptance by the public of a joint system wherein a city now served by three VHF channels may eventually add three or four more in the UHF.

There is a historical parallel in the case of AM. In many communities there are AM stations authorized to transmit with 50,000 watts of radiated power; in most, there are stations operating with 5,000 watts; and in practically every city and hamlet in the nation there are one or more 250 watters. These are generally known as "Clear Channels," "Regional Channels," and "Local" or "Community Channels." It is generally accepted that this is a logical step in the future development of television.

Color Television

One of the more controversial developments in television is color. There can be little doubt that it is a superior medium, and that it will eventually embrace most television transmission. Heavy cost, and lack of additional revenues to offset the costs is largely the reason for slow development.

Historically, CBS Laboratories developed a cheap and highly efficient color TV system during the "freeze." CBS was prepared to go all-out to install and market its system. Essentially, it achieved high-fidelity color through the use of a mechanical whirling disc after the fashion of the physicist Benham's "top" invention of the early 19th century. No one can truthfully say it is not a good system, nor that it does not create beautiful, and faithful, color pictures. The basic problem, the FCC finally decided, was that the system was "incompatible." That is to say, it could not be superimposed upon the then existing television system so that tens of millions of TV receivers in the hands of the public could continue to receive clear monochrome pictures while the CBS color signals were being transmitted.

Accordingly, a compatible all-electronic color system was developed and adopted. It is enormously expensive. Consequently, the public has not so far bought more expensive color receivers in sufficient quantity to warrant large-scale color outlays by advertisers. Few station operators have been able to afford to speculate on large color programming or equipment in the absence of audience and revenue potential. It's the same "chicken and egg" cycle all over again.

RCA, with a virtual monopoly of color TV manufacturing patents, has poured hundreds of millions into development of receivers, and into the color programming of its subsidiary network,

NBC. It's at least an interesting parallel of the old "music box" pattern of a full generation earlier.

Indications are that competitive entry into the color receiver field by other majors, such as Zenith, Motorola, Philco, and others, will result in better sets at lower prices. When the public can buy replacement color sets at prices comparable to black-and-white, the color boom will be on. New advertising budgets, based on the mass appeal of color-oriented products, will undoubtedly bring about a new economic cycle in television comparable to that of the 50's.

Station operators will, by and large, convert to color as soon as competitive pressures become a major factor. Nevertheless, the huge backlog of monochrome film, produced for theatre exhibition and for television, will continue to be a major TV program factor for an indefinite time. Most TV film production is switching to color negatives for "futures"; but Hollywood continues to use black-and-white for most low budget pictures.

REGULATION

One of the most frequent questions raised about broadcasting and its future concerns the nature of Federal regulation and its long-term effect upon business conditions.

We have already seen how the FCC has developed into a sort of quasi-judicial, quasi-legislative body. It is an administrative and enforcement arm of Congress, with its members selected by the President. It is required to have no more than four members of the President's political faith and three of the opposition party.

Interpretations of the Communications Act by the FCC have varied so widely over the years that there has been no real pattern of regulation. The enormous expansion in the use of radio frequencies for all sorts of non-broadcasting, non-military purposes, has left the FCC with a staggering burden of administrative paper. Merely renewing over a million separate licenses yearly is an impossible task even with no review at all.

The result is that the FCC and its staff are so badly backed up in work load that careful consideration of many matters is out of the question. This in turn sometimes leads to the application of theories with unwarranted conclusions in the regulation of commercial stations.

So confused is the issue now that the Federal Communications Bar Association has recently completed a committee study recommending drastic changes in the structure of the Commission and the law itself.

Basically these recommendations call for four major changes:

1) Replacement of the FCC altogether by a new structure consisting of an Administrator; a communications court resembling the tax court; and a five-man policy-making commission.

2) Elimination of the "equal-time" political rules and other regulations of political broadcasting from the Act.

3) Amendment of the "no censorship" provisions of the Act to ban FCC judgment or evaluation as to the public interest in the composition, nature, or character of the programs broadcast.

4) Modernization of the common carrier regulations.

These recommendations in themselves sum up most of the regulatory problems facing the industry.

The Commission is periodically concerned with both the economics and the content of broadcasting. In the former category, there is no direct legal authorization for this concern; and in the latter category it is specifically prohibited by law. Nevertheless, these are two of the favorite areas of activity by the FCC and the countless study groups, committees, and investigations that it conducts.

There is good reason for this confusion, since the FCC is charged by Congress with licensing use of the air waves "in the public interest, convenience, and necessity." But no one has ever adequately explained what that means.

Almost of necessity, the FCC argues, it must establish some guidelines for what is acceptable and what is unacceptable programming in order for it to arrive at any judgment of what is in the "public interest, convenience, and necessity."

Dissonant voices claim that the "traffic cop" role, to prevent stations from interfering with one another is the only legal function. Others—including most Commissioners—interpret this to mean that they are also a "watchdog" of the public's entertainment fare. Accordingly, there is practiced a form of subtle and indirect censorship, in that a licensee is told that he had better be prepared to defend his own interpretation of what is the local public interest if he wants to get his license renewed.

On the economic side, the Commission has consistently interpreted its Congressional charge to develop a "fully competitive nationwide system" to mean as many broadcasting stations and networks as possible. The argument about whether too many stations deteriorate the public interest through a sort of Gresham's Law of broadcasting is as old as the FCC. Occasionally the FCC takes this course, as in the current studies of "birth control" on radio outlets. But historically, the FCC looks upon any less than four networks, or less than four stations in a given market area as a "monopoly," although it has no specific authorization to be concerned with monopoly.

The public debate—fanned to fever pitch by continued and unfriendly coverage by the print media—over former Chairman Newton Minow's now famous "vast wasteland" speech is still raging. Many people have virtually written off broadcasting's future prospects because of it. But this was merely another case of history repeating itself.

At one time, during the Chairmanship of James Lawrence Fly, the FCC published the "Blue Book" which purported to tell a broadcaster—in extraordinary detail—what he could and could not do. It laid out specifications for commercial content, purported to define what was and was not in the public interest. It specifically eliminated from a "public service" category any program that had a commercial sponsor, regardless of the worth or intent of the program.

This was a much more virulent attempt at regulation and censorship than has even been attempted in recent years. It was beaten down by the broadcasters themselves through appeals to Congress.

Regularly, the FCC, on economic injury grounds, attempts to bring under federal regulation the three television networks. Two things have regularly foiled these attempts:

1) The fear on the part of Congress that the FCC would then have absolute censorship power over networks, which it can now exercise only through licensing of any stations owned by a network company.

2) The continual growth of the medium resulting in the elimination of the "hardship" case of the third network.

It seems reasonable to expect that the FCC will eventually

adopt rules to limit the amount of time which an individual station can turn over to a national network for programming.

The objective—and one of the likely results—of such further regulations would be to put back in business dozens of independent program packagers and producers, who have fallen by the wayside in recent years through the drying up of their market. Whether such a change is desirable remains to be seen. From the practical viewpoint of station operation, it is largely unnecessary. It would at the same time cause a tremendous hardship on very small market stations who must have network service to stay alive, while it would liberate for direct sale at higher net prices a large amount of time in large markets—time which is now pretty well controlled by the networks.

A recent phenomenon in regulation has been the effort by the FCC to air the complaints of the public about local station operation via community-wide "hearings." These are not hearings in the usual sense of the word: a contest for award of a license or a renewal. These are hearings in mid-term of a station's license to see what, if anything, the public thinks about its TV stations.

The most recent excursion into this extra-legal procedure was a hearing in Omaha, Nebraska, in which the local stations were praised, and the FCC was roundly denounced, by dozens of witnesses, and even by a unanimous resolution of the Nebraska legislature. It appears doubtful that this type of "hearing" will be attempted in the same form again.

Licenses are granted for a three-year term, and most generally are renewed without undue commotion. The FCC does demand, however, that the licensee make a showing that he has scrupulously fulfilled the statements made in his last license renewal application with respect to program balance, commercial content, treatment of controversial issues, and the like. Normally the prudent, fair-minded, and successful operator has no trouble with this procedure.

NETWORKS

Perhaps the most familiar feature of television, and the least understood, is the network. In the largest sense of the word, there are three of them—ABC, CBS, and NBC—each with about 200 affiliated stations, and each supplying programs and revenue in large degree to about 120 stations.

A network is many things to many people: to a small station operator in a city of 25,000, it is his only hope of survival; to a large market station operator it can be the difference between a break-even and a large profit; to a seller of direct national or "spot" advertising, it is anathema; to the FCC's economic study groups it is "monopoly"; to the FCC it is one of the biggest station licensees that must be regulated; to the majority of the public, it is the source of entertainment, news, and historic events that could never have been available to the average man during several lifetimes of travel and exposure. A network is, in short, a basic necessity of television. If it were abolished by law tomorrow, groups of station operators would invent it all over again under a different name the day after tomorrow.

A network, reduced to its simplest terms, is a confederation of stations that can look to a common focal point for the creation, production, distribution, and sale of programs.

The four great radio networks were roughly similar to the television networks. A combination of many factors made radio networks almost obsolete. First of all, the proliferation of stations made it a necessity for thousands of them to program without a network, since there simply were not enough networks to go around. Nor were any more of them economically feasible. Secondly, the advertising power of television so overshadowed radio that the networks could not sell their product. The combination of these forces made AM radio become primarily a locally programmed medium, each station beaming its particular type of program to a minority to whom it could appeal. National advertisers were no longer attracted to the splintered national network market, and radio networks almost died.

Technical developments, including low cost tape recorders, inexhaustible supplies of recorded music, and the ability to operate a small radio station with a handful of people and minute expenditures, made the era of the independent radio station the norm rather than the exception. Radio networks became syndicated news program suppliers rather than networks in the original sense of the word. Station payments for carrying network commercials disappeared entirely in some cases, and a whole new concept developed in AM radio.

Networks have never been a factor in FM, although there are now some program supplier organizations called by the name "network" that do trade programs for exposure in order to sell "class" advertising.

In television, the situation is quite different. There is simply not in existence the physical and economic means to program three or four competitive TV services without the network system.

Typically a network will provide programming as much as 14 hours out of an 18-hour broadcast day, requiring the individual licensee to provide only the limited amount of local interest programming, news, and special events, which it is uniquely qualified to perform in each city. The network, on its part, sells advertising in connection with its programs to be exposed on all or the major part of its affiliated stations. Its charges for this time are the aggregate of the charges for each station broadcasting the program or commercial.

A typical network affiliation contract will provide that the station waives any payment for the first 20 to 30 hours per month of network commercial programs in order to defray the cost of distribution via AT&T radio relay facilities. After that "free hours" minimum, the station will typically receive 30% of the gross charges made by the network to the advertiser for each commercial segment.

A median breakdown of revenues will show that a station will probably receive about 30% of its total revenue from its network source, in addition to the value in audience attraction of the network's programs. An additional 30% to 40% will be derived from advertising sold to local or regional customers, and the remainder will come from sale of advertising directly to national advertisers—the so-called "national spot."

The concern of the FCC for controlling network practices stems from the supposition that the dependence of the licensee on his network for service and revenue makes him something less than a free agent. He may, according to the FCC, have abdicated his licensee responsibility by providing to the network the bulk of his program time.

FCC economists are fond of describing this situation as the

"network monopoly." When confronted by the fact that there were two networks which controlled most of the shows and most of the money they called it a "duopoly." Now that the third network, the American Broadcasting Company, is a fully competitive factor, the situation is described as an "oligopoly." With the FCC's preoccupation for the addition of a fourth network source, one may be excused for speculating on what it will be called, when and if it becomes economically feasible.

It is a safe assumption that if all networks were abolished by government fiat, the station operators themselves would invent a replacement that would largely duplicate the present facilities for pooling the cost and speculative selling of huge program commitments and nationwide advertising exposure.

In the almost unique relationship between networks and stations there could be no networks without the enthusiastic endorsement of individual stations. Conversely, there would doubtless be far fewer stations in operation than there are if there had been no networks.

A reduction in the number of hours a station might be permitted to broadcast network programs raises some interesting speculation. In the first place, there is the question whether such a limitation is constitutional under the First Amendment, or at best, consonant with the Communications Act insofar as it involves a direct federal limitation on program material itself. Additionally the question is raised as to the possibility of continued existence for many stations in small towns and sparsely settled areas. And finally, it is almost a certainty that group buying and cost-sharing practices would spring up among stations to provide that programming which would no longer be available from the network source. Whether this would have a beneficial effect in spreading the responsibility for, and the economic benefits of, program production is a moot question.

OTHER TV PROGRAM SOURCES

The bulk of program hours not provided to stations from network sources has in the past been supplied by seemingly inexhaustible reservoirs of motion picture features originally made for theater exhibition. These movies have not only provided the comedians and the columnists with endless gags about their age, they have also enabled a whole new generation to catch up on the Hollywood output of the 30's and 40's. They have been a godsend to stations where bulk programming was needed, but they are frequently so expensive that a station might have to use one show seven times in order to recover its money.

This backlog of Hollywood productions is fast being exhausted, however. Not only have they been consumed in the insatiable maw of television at a rapid rate, but the production of Hollywood, numerically speaking, has taken a drastic drop since 1950. Accordingly there is simply not the feature film product available to keep on supplying television indefinitely.

Another result of the competition of television has been to push Hollywood into more daring themes, more "adult" treatments, and quite frankly, more salacious or downright risque material. The question is legitimately raised whether more than a small fraction of today's Hollywood movies are suitable for indiscriminate transmission into the home.

The foregoing will, without government prodding, require the development of some totally new program forms and concepts.

"Syndicated" film production for television at one time reached a very prolific output. This largely comprised half-hour film series in the action-adventure, wild west, situation comedy, and detective fiction fields. These films were sold directly to stations or to advertisers for placement on stations in non-network time periods. Gradually, however, as the costs rose and the network time expanded, the syndicators by and large found themselves with no customers except the networks themselves. As a result there are very few, if any, new syndicated series of programs being manufactured especially for non-network or "spot" sale. Practically all syndication product is being produced for, and financed by, one of the networks.

Most if not all the film series used by the networks are, sooner or later, put out for syndication sale as "off-network reruns." In some instances these programs have not been shown at all in a particular market because the network time had been pre-empted there. In such a case the syndicator gets a higher price for the "residual" right to use the film than if it is an actual rerun.

The pricing structure for film is a function of free market economics. Some cities have a station with unlimited resources which will pay the asking price for practically every film that comes along, thus creating a shortage for the competition. In other markets all the stations bargain closely, thus driving the average sale price for syndicated shows or features well below the offered price. Once a program has been sponsored for a season on network, the syndicated rerun price is practically all profit to the syndicator except for direct sales costs.

Reruns are a much misunderstood program form. Most film programs are produced at a cost many times greater than can be recovered by the initial sale to a network or other advertiser. Therefore, it is usual practice to program 39 originals and 13 repeats during a typical 52 week run. Thus, each program could theoretically be priced at 75% of cost with a resulting 100% recovery at the end of the first year. The pricing is usually much lower than 75%, however, and the final amortization of cost and profit, if any, results from the resale of the "residual" rights in the program after its initial exposure.

Reruns are therefore a plain economic necessity if television is to be supplied with any new product at all. A typical three-station television market programs an aggregate of over 20,000 hours per year! There is simply not that much program material in existence, drawing on all sources, without reruns.

A highly popular program has little need for sale of "residuals" until after it has completed a three- or four-year first run. On the other hand, a program which has a low tune-in rating will usually go into syndication almost at once. The fewer the viewers on the first run, the larger potential new audience it will have on its repeat runs. After all, any program is a "rerun" only to those who have seen it. To everyone else it is an entirely new program. People who tune out the summer rerun of a popular series of the past year will usually watch another rerun which is to them a new program.

Has anyone ever seriously considered consigning Gershwin to the trash heap because he has already been heard?

The turn-over rate of the television audience makes reruns necessary if there is to be anything approaching saturation of the potential audience for each show. The best proof of this theory is that most network programs have experienced larger measured audiences on their reruns than they did in their original showings.

There is no universal formula for successful locally-produced programs. Some very inexpensive programs with local personalities attract a huge audience and remain commercially successful for years. Others, with high-priced talent and elaborate production lay elaborate eggs. High technical costs severely restrict the quantity of live studio production in most stations.

Where stations attract their most consistent and loyal audiences in local programming is in the news field, together with direct coverage of local professional and college sporting events.

PAY TELEVISION

Periodically there is a flurry of activity in pay-as-you-see television. Such a system, using the broadcast channels, can potentially be a medium of almost unimaginable revenue proportions. Today a World Series telecast might be seen, at least in part, by upwards of 100,000,000 people. If a mere 20 million were to have to pay only $1.00 for the privilege, that one game would outstrip the revenue potential of the entire baseball season for the teams involved and the broadcasting promoter. The combinations are endless.

The one flaw in the theory is that if the FCC were to turn over the present broadcast channels to pay-TV in such a way that the World Series example were possible, then any and all box office attractions would obviously hold back from advertising-supported free TV in order to cash in on the pay-TV bonanza. At the risk of destroying the free medium, the Congress has given no indication of its willingness to allow the FCC to do this.

There are at present two experimental broadcast pay-TV systems in operation. There is some thinking on the Commission that this effort should be expanded, but only in the high UHF channels.

Pay-TV may become a practical reality with no FCC jurisdiction, providing the program service is fed to home receivers over a wire or cable system. This may yet be a practical approach to the matter. Its biggest limitation is that it is so much more expensive than broadcasting.

From a practical political viewpoint, pay-TV becomes a "rich man's medium," while the present system is equally available to everyone with a set, regardless of means. This is the most powerful deterrent in Congress to the widespread adoption by the FCC of a broadcast pay-TV system.

Should either form of pay-TV, wired or broadcast, appear to

be an imminent practical reality, most broadcasters would enter the field immediately through conversion of all or part of their present service to a subscription fee system.

FUTURE DEVELOPMENTS

The transistor and miniaturized circuits have already revolutionized the technical state of broadcasting in the past few years. "Transistors" are amplifying devices which operate in a tiny blob of solid state plastic rather than with redhot filaments inside a glass vacuum tube. The vacuum tube is all but doomed by the transistor. The advantages are readily apparent: it is tiny; it requires very little power input; it creates no heat; it requires no maintenance; it is virtually indestructible; it is cheap.

The transistor has already made possible an enormous increase in radio listening. Everyone is familiar with the sight of a glazed-eyed teenager walking down the street or riding in a bus listening to his favorite rock 'n' roll artist. Tiny transistorized portables are the constant companion of listeners in every conceivable place, and during every sort of activity.

Tiny portable pick-up, recording, and broadcast equipment has permitted radio, and television too, to provide on-the-scene reports of every form of human endeavor. This will increase, particularly in television, as miniaturized camera, videotape, and transmission equipment rolls out of the laboratories.

Automatic machinery of every conceivable type can be applied to broadcasting, and will be increasingly employed. For example, it is possible to make separately programmed FM self-supporting and profitable by use of automatic long-playing audio tape machines and automatic logging procedures.

WKRC-TV, Cincinnati, has already demonstrated the feasibility of a fully automated TV operation. Activated by a perforated paper tape, computors perform every one of the day-to-day functions of selection and switching of audio and visual program sources. The result is a tremendous saving in technical manpower, one of the highest expense items in a TV station.

Electronic light amplification will one day replace the electron tube as the picture element in television. This will enable the home viewer to see a wall screen picture as large as he desires—or as large as he can afford. This will in due time be available in color, and most of the program material on it will be color.

"Talk back" circuits, to enable the home viewer to signify his opinion of a program, buy a product, or take part in a political poll, are already past the initial laboratory stage. This development will put a strange twist on George Orwell. Already everyone is being watched by "Big Brother," but American industrial genius is going, sooner or later, to make it possible to give "Big Brother" some back-talk.

In a continually changing pattern to meet the needs and desires of the American people, broadcasting in all its forms will follow and adapt itself to the tremendous population increase forecast for the next few decades.

In a communications system of immeasurable complexity and unparalleled rate of growth, the past is merely prologue.

CHAPTER 2

Acquiring a Television Station

BY EDWARD WETTER

Edwin Tornberg & Company

A graduate of the University of Michigan where he obtained both his Bachelor's and Master's degrees, Mr. Wetter served with the Army for five years during and after World War II, and thereafter spent 11 years with the Federal Government, becoming Director of Special Operations for the Assistant Secretary of Defense for Research and Engineering before resigning to enter private industry. Mr. Wetter has been a broker in mass communication media for the past six years and is now associated with Edwin Tornberg & Company, New York, as Vice President.

A BROKER, according to Webster, is "one who acts as agent or middleman for another." As in almost all endeavors, the brokerage business has become highly specialized. A large stock brokerage house has different analysts for common stock, for bonds, for debentures and so on. The real estate broker tends to deal in specific types of land or buildings. In the same way, specialists have developed who deal primarily in properties concerned with mass communications.

The goal of any broker is to find the price and terms at which an owner is willing to sell and a prospective purchaser is willing to buy. The more complex the economic and sociological ramifications of a given enterprise are, the more experienced and knowledgeable the broker must be. In the case of broadcast properties, the situation is complicated further since he is involved in a field which is in a constant state of rapid change, is subject to federal regulation, and must be responsive to technological improvements and public needs.

Thus, the station broker must be conversant with the policies and objectives of the Federal Communications Commission (FCC), have an understanding of cultural and economic trends, attain a knowledge of many legal and accounting procedures, and become acquainted with the many technological developments affecting the broadcast industry.

Ownership of a broadcast property is attainable only by purchasing an existing facility or by applying to the FCC for a permit to build a new one. Suffice it to say here that the procedures involved in obtaining such a construction permit are an extremely difficult and time-consuming undertaking. In this chapter we are, then, concerned with the acquisition of a broadcast facility by purchase, and the role of the station broker is such a transaction.

THE GROWTH OF BROADCASTING

The dynamic character of the television industry has manifest itself over the years in many different ways and can be demonstrated most clearly by the phenomenal growth it has enjoyed. An important index of this growth is the dollar volume of commercial TV time sold to advertisers.

Not only has the dollar volume of television time sales increased year by year but the number of stations has grown dramatically as well. According to figures compiled by the FCC, the number of commercial television stations as of May 31, 1963, was as follows:

Licensed (on the air)	518
Construction Permits on the air (new stations)	60
Construction Permits not on the air (new stations)	85
Total Authorized Stations	663

(Of the 578 operating television stations on May 31, 1963, 486 were VHF and 92 UHF.)

The foregoing has shown the vast size of the still growing television broadcasting industry, but what about the turnover in station ownership? The two most significant statistics in this regard are the number of stations that change hands and the dollar volume

TELEVISION TIME SALES—1948-1962*
(In millions of dollars)

Year	National Network	National Non-Network	Local	Total	Per cent Increase Over Previous Year
1948 †	$ 2.5	—	$ 6.2	$ 8.7	—
1949	10.8	$ 7.3	9.5	27.5	—
1950	35.2	25.0	30.4	90.6	229.2
1951	97.6	59.7	51.3	208.6	130.2
1952	137.7	80.2	65.2	283.1	35.7
1953	171.9	124.3	88.5	384.7	35.9
1954	241.2	176.8	120.1	538.1	39.9
1955	308.9	222.4	149.8	681.1	26.6
1956	367.7	281.2	174.2	823.1	20.8
1957	394.2	300.5	174.0	868.7	5.5
1958	424.5	345.2	181.3	951.0	9.5
1959	445.8	424.2	200.6	1070.6	12.6
1960	471.6	459.2	215.8	1146.6	7.1
1961	480.3	468.5	211.2	1160.0	1.2
1962	514.3	528.7	233.9	1276.9	10.1

* Extracted from table in *Broadcasting*, Volume 64, No. 7; February 18, 1963. Original figures from the FCC except 1962 figures estimated by *Broadcasting*.
† In 1948, FCC reported only "total revenues" (from time, talent and services) from "network programs" and from business "sold directly by stations." Hence, figures for that first year of television financial reporting are not comparable with figures for time sales in ensuing years.

of the transactions. The latter figure is especially significant for the broker since his commission is based on the price that the station brings.

In computing the number of stations in the trading, an AM-FM facility was counted as one radio unit; an AM-only or FM-only transaction similarly was counted as one radio unit. Dollar volume figures represent total considerations reported for all transactions, whether majority or minority interests were involved. In many transactions involving joint radio-television properties, individual values were not assigned to the radio and television stations. Such sales are reported in the column headed "Combined Radio-TV."

Thus, the more than 3,000 radio and television stations that changed ownership over the past nine years brought in excess of $950 million. Of this total, some 364 transactions involving over $553 million included a television facility.

NUMBER OF STATIONS AND DOLLAR VOLUME
OF STATION TRADING*

(Volume given in millions of dollars)

Year	Radio Only		Combined Radio-TV		TV Only		Total	
	No.	Vol.	No.	Vol.	No.	Vol.	No.	Vol.
1954	187	$10.2	18	$26.2	27	$23.9	232	$60.3
1955	242	27.3	11	22.4	29	23.4	282	73.1
1956	316	32.6	24	65.2	21	17.8	361	115.6
1957	357	48.2	28	47.5	38	28.5	423	124.2
1958	407	49.9	17	60.9	23	16.8	447	127.5
1959	436	65.5	15	42.7	21	15.2	472	123.5
1960	345	51.8	10	24.6	21	22.9	376	99.3
1961	282	55.5	13	42.1	24	31.2	319	128.8
1962	306	59.9	8	18.8	16	23.0	330	101.7
Totals	2878	400.9	144	350.4	220	202.8	3242	954.1

* Compiled from tables on pages 100 and 102; *Broadcasting,* Volume 64, No. 7, February 18, 1963.

AVAILABILITY OF PROPERTIES

As we have seen, the number of stations that have changed hands in recent years and the prices that they have commanded are large indeed in their totality. Yet, there is a great variation in the worth of individual properties. A television station can range in value anywhere from $250,000 to more than $20,000,000.

And so, too, do the prospective purchasers range greatly in their financial situation, their backgrounds, their needs and their capabilities. The more informed the client is about the industry, the more he understands the high prices broadcast facilities command. Present station owners and top executives constitute the greatest number of prospective purchasers a national media broker is likely to have. On the other hand, the desirability of owning such a highly respected and usually profitable enterprise also attracts other industries wishing to diversify their holdings. The present station owner wants to own more stations or move into larger markets; the large company with surplus capital wishes to invest its money in a growing and vital industry. There are very few individuals with sufficient funds to purchase top market television stations. The broker's real problem is to find good facilities to sell at reasonable prices, for he has many more prospective buyers than available properties.

Several new rules of the FCC and its recent tightening of control over the industry had been expected to affect adversely the selling market. The FCC has imposed many fines, has revoked several licenses, has evidenced a desire for more and more program control, and has had license renewal hearings in several cities. The recent three-year rule provides that an owner must show conclusive and acceptable reasons before he can sell his station unless he has owned it for at least three years. Nonetheless, a seller's market still exists. It must be remembered that no individual or company may own more than five VHF and two UHF television stations. Furthermore, most available VHF-TV channels have been assigned —certainly almost all of those that could be constructed in the larger markets. At the same time, our population continues to grow; our gross national product continues to rise, and our labor force continues to strive for shorter work weeks and thus, more leisure time, all of which tend to make television more profitable a business. Present station owners realize this all too well, and so, we find a trend toward long-term holdings and fewer short-term capital gain investors.

In spite of this fact, a considerable number of highly desirable properties become available for purchase each year. Some reasons for selling might be a wish to retire, the failure of a son to be interested in the business, sickness, or the desire to obtain a more important facility in a larger market. Underlying all these reasons, however, is the cold hard fact that almost all broadcast facilities can be sold today for a price well in excess of the original investment. Our tax laws provide that the profit thus received is taxable at a maximum rate of 25%, a considerable inducement to sell, in this day of high personal income taxes.

Criteria for Purchase

Contrary to widespread belief, there is no general yardstick that can be used to determine the worth of a particular broadcast facility. Each property is unique and must be analyzed individually. In evaluating a given station, many separate factors must be considered and collated to reach a realistic picture. The most important general factors are: the market, the technical facility, personnel and financial requirements.

The Market: There is much we must learn about a given market so that we may view the situation as it pertains to broadcasting. Size and growth history of population, consumer spendable income, number of television homes, audience listening habits, amount and type of competition, and many other facts must be garnered and analyzed. We must check the FCC for any pending applications for the construction of new facilities and judge the effect this may have on the market. We must look at future trends in population growth and the types and number of industries that provide the economic base of the community. We must look at the prejudices and attitudes of the local population to gauge the acceptability of the prospective new owner. As a general rule, the larger the market and the less keen the competition, the more desirable and valuable the property.

The Technical Facility: With the exception of a few all UHF areas, the really desirable TV stations broadcast on VHF channels (2 through 13). We are most interested to ascertain the actual coverage of the population with a first-class video and audio signal. Information as to the exact contours of this coverage can be obtained from the FCC where engineering maps are on file. The station must provide the FCC periodic "proofs of performance" to demonstrate that they are broadcasting in accordance with the engineering specifications they filed with the FCC. The transmitter site and studios must be inspected to determine the type, amount, and condition of the equipment. Most prospective purchasers hire a consulting engineer for this purpose and also to advise them as to newer and more desirable equipment that would improve the operation. Technological advances in this field have been rapid and dramatic, videotape being one good example. We must compare the technical capabilities of the station in question with the other stations covering the market so as to assess properly the competitive position of each.

Personnel: When purchasing a radio or TV property, you do not just buy wires and tubes or buildings and land. You buy a going concern which succeeds or fails depending on the caliber of the people who run the operation. They are all important—the manager, the program director, the performers, the sales staff and even the traffic girl, the bookkeeper and the secretary. An attractive, efficient receptionist can be a very valuable asset. A broadcast operation is the sum total of the staff.

Financing: All of the above, even at its best, is of far less value if adequate funds are not available for proper management. Time and again, potentially fine facilities have failed to realize their potential because of inadequate capital. Some have managed to succeed in spite of a lack of funds, but this is a difficult and long road to follow and requires exceptional talent.

After the general factors have been weighed and assessed, we must look at the specific station involved. Two diverse approaches can be made. The first is based primarily on the actual past performance of the station in question. The second approach depends chiefly upon the expectancy of future earnings and operational prospects in light of present management, competition and market conditions.

The first method is most sound when applied to a market that is more or less static, that has had little change in the competitive situation, and that has not had any dramatic population growth. Coupled with this, the station in question should have a rather stable gross and earnings history under sound management. In other words, no substantial upward change, other than that of normal progress, can be realistically expected. When basing the fair market value of the station primarily on past performance, the most useful index is the price-earnings ratio, that is, the quotient of price divided by earnings after taxes. In a recent study completed by our firm, the sales of 72 television stations during the period from 1950 through 1959 were analyzed. The average price-earnings ratio for those stations for which earnings data were available was 15.39; that is, those stations on average commanded a price of 15.39 times their annual earnings after taxes. Many considerations weighed heavily on this average, however, particularly the definition of what truly constitutes earnings, the market conditions, the value of land and buildings included in the sale, and the like.

Another useful method in such an evaluation is the study of prices paid for similar stations in similar markets. Unfortunately, there are always important dissimilarities, and often details on recent comparable sales are not available. Thus, even these yardsticks, helpful as they are, are tenuous at best.

Often, the potential of a station is far greater than that realized by the owner. In such cases, past performances cannot be the basic criteria, and the evaluation must perforce be made with far greater emphasis on the analysis of the general factors discussed above.

A TYPICAL CASE HISTORY

It is difficult to deal with the complex subject of station evaluation in the abstract. A specific case in point will perhaps more clearly demonstrate the kind of thinking that must enter into the analysis of the worth of a property. The following is an example from a typical report that would be prepared for a prospective buyer:

> The general picture, therefore, resolves itself to the fact that the market revenue is there and that the only competitor has greatly outdistanced the present management of W-TV. The present owner of W-TV spends over five months a year in Florida. When he is in the east, he does not reside in the city in which he owns the TV station, and devotes practically all of his time to his numerous other enterprises. He has an excellent income from these investments outside of the broadcasting field and frankly admits that he has had no desire to increase gross or earnings at W-TV since most of such an increase would have to be paid in taxes. He has, therefore, been content to let W-TV run itself for many years, has devoted little time or attention to the station, and has done literally nothing by way of advertising and promoting the facility. W-TV has a gross income of only a fraction of that of its competitor.
>
> The most serious defects of the present operation can be corrected by efficient management and basic revisions in programming. Local programming can be very much improved particularly with regard to news coverage. Insofar as network programming is concerned, re-scheduling and better selection of programs should be undertaken at once. The sales manager should be replaced immediately and the entire department re-organized. Details of the improvements that can be made and a seven-year projection of income and earnings under new effective management are given in Appendix "A." [An appendix of this kind would be a part of the actual report, but limitations of space preclude its inclusion here.]
>
> There is an excellent chance that the current application to

change the transmitter site and increase the tower height of W-TV will be approved by the FCC. Such a move would greatly increase the coverage and reduce the present reception difficulties. This would give a truly competitive stature to W-TV and significantly enhance the possibilities of obtaining a fair share of the TV advertising dollar being spent in the market.

The network affiliation is in no jeopardy since this is a two station market and since there is little likelihood that a third, let alone a fourth, TV station will be allocated to this area in the foreseeable future.

For details on personnel, ratings, coverage, rate structure, network and local programming, equipment and plant, please see Appendix "B." [Such an appendix would be included in an actual report.]

The past history of W-TV and the competitor, the significant operating improvements that can be made, the likely increase in coverage and quality of signal, and the conditions of the market all indicate a real opportunity to bring about dramatic increases in the gross and earnings of W-TV. In essence, then, the potential of W-TV looms as one of the most attractive that we have come across in recent years. Under these circumstances, the asking price seems not only reasonable, but a wise and prudent business investment.

A similar assessment must be made in varying degrees for every station the conscientious broker undertakes to sell. For the most part, a written report is not necessary, particularly when dealing with an individual rather than the representative of a large firm or a syndicate.

SUMMARY

The broker functions in three basic ways: assisting the owner in his decision as to the price and terms he can reasonably hope to get, presenting a complete and realistic assessment of the situation to the prospective purchaser, and negotiating the actual sale so as to effect a fair and equitable transaction for both principals.

It is essential that the reputable broker treat the information received from both seller and buyer in the strictest confidence possible. The seller does not want to upset his staff or give his competition an advantage during the period of negotiations, which frequently can become quite lengthy. He obviously does not want the details of his financial situation and the intimate operations of his station to fall into the wrong hands. In most cases, he does not even wish the fact that he is entertaining the idea of selling to become generally known. The broker must, therefore, exercise extreme caution in selecting those clients to whom he will present the facts concerning the availability of a specific property. He must first be certain that the station meets the basic requirements of the buyer in terms of location, facility, market size and price range.

Once the buyer has been apprised of all the factual information available and has decided, together with the broker, that he has a bona fide interest in pursuing the matter further, an initial meeting is arranged with the owner. If the latter is satisfied as to the qualifications and sincerity of the buyer, arrangements are made for an inspection of the facilities and an audit of the books. If both principals are satisfied at this point, detailed negotiations as to the conditions of the sale are undertaken. A great variety of questions must be answered, including tax considerations, security provisions, and the like. Once the specific terms of the purchase have been agreed upon, the transaction is turned over to the respective attorneys who jointly prepare the sales contract. Throughout this period, the broker is consulted frequently and must often find the solution to unique and knotty problems.

After execution of the final contract, the principals have 30 days in which to file the contract and special forms with the FCC requesting the transfer of the license. No sale can be finalized until after FCC approval, and then the actual transfer of the station to the new licensee must be made within 45 days.

It usually takes four to eight weeks from the time a prospective purchaser first learns of the availability of a property until a final contract is prepared and executed. The preparation of the application to the FCC usually takes another two weeks. The FCC has established a waiting period of 30 days before it will consider an application. During this time, the FCC staff is preparing its recommendations for the Commission and the station owner must advertise twice a week for two weeks, both on the air and in a local newspaper, that the station is seeking a transfer of the license from the FCC. This is done to apprise the public that a broadcast facility is changing hands and thus permit anyone with objections to such a transfer to inform the FCC. Obviously, only valid and reasonable objections are given serious consideration by the Commission.

Because of the heavy work load of the FCC staff, it is seldom possible for the Commission to consider an application for transfer as soon as the required 30-day waiting period is over. On an average, such approval takes six to eight weeks providing everything is in perfect order and the FCC staff has no questions concerning this transaction. Should the latter be the case, the staff will request all the additional information it needs to render a sound recommendation to the Commission. Although such delays seem exasperating to all parties directly concerned, it is necessary that the public interest be protected.

Frequently the broker's final appearance is at the "closing," that is, the actual transfer of the property. Even at this late date, he may be called upon to arbitrate differences in the interpretation of important provisions of the contract. The broker has completed his task only after the station has actually changed hands. However, a knowledgeable broker often is retained by the new owner in a consulting capacity to advise on changing market conditions, programming, technological advances, management practices and future acquisitions.

Assuming that everything goes smoothly, that the purchaser's initial interest in the property continues, and that the seller remains satisfied with the prospective buyer and the handling of the negotiations, the following "time-table" sums up the basic steps in purchasing a broadcast facility.

Steps	*Normal Time Consumed*
1. Examination of data supplied by broker	2-4 weeks
2. Initial meetings with seller	1-3 days
3. Inspection of facility and market	2-4 days
4. Detailed negotiations on price and terms	1-3 days
5. Audit of books and engineering survey	1-2 weeks
6. Preparation and execution of contract of sale	2-4 weeks
7. Preparation and filing of FCC forms	1-3 weeks
8. Approval of transfer by FCC	5-8 weeks
9. Actual transfer of property	15-45 days
Normal Total Time Consumed	3-6 months

There are many places along this sensitive and often tortuous route where negotiations bog down and all too often terminate. In this case, we must present the buyer with other availabilities and must find a new purchaser for the station. Obviously, the disappointments are many, but the rewards for success are great.

We have looked at the many diversified fields with which the station broker must be familiar. Only by remaining thoroughly conversant with all these facets can he properly provide his vital and unique service to the broadcast industry.

PART TWO

MANAGING THE TELEVISION STATION

CHAPTER 3

The Network-
Affiliated Station

BY MILTON D. FRIEDLAND

Plains Television Stations, Springfield, Illinois

A graduate of Roosevelt College, Chicago, Mr. Friedland has been an instructor in that city at the Moser Business College, the De Paul University School of Commerce and the Northwestern University School of Commerce. He began his television career in sales service capacities for WBKB and then WBBM-TV in Chicago, moving to Springfield, Illinois, in 1953 where he is now Vice President and General Manager of the Plains Television Stations group, WICS-WCHU-WICD, in Springfield-Champaign-Danville.

MANAGEMENT of a television station involves the operation of a complex business that functions 365 days a year, and often 17 hours a day or longer. The industry itself is one of the fastest growing of any in the United States. Today, television is found in about 93% of wired American homes; the number of TV homes has climbed to almost 51 million with approximately 59 million television sets; the public has invested almost $21 billion in TV sets since telecasting began; and there were 579 commercial television stations plus 75 non-commercial educational stations operating in almost 340 cities in the United States as of December, 1963. Moreover, national advertising billings place television in the forefront of all media, and the spiral continues upward.

Furthermore, television is the most rapid-changing of all media. The obsolescence of equipment brought about by sharp technical advances, the development of new program concepts to meet insatiable audience tastes, the various attitudes of public

53

opinion, and the tensions of government pressure all present top management with recurrent challenges.

Television, in fact, is assuming its role as the most potent communications force in all history. We spend more hours watching television than in any other waking occupation except working. Our children focus more time and attention on television than on anything else except school classroom work. The hearth is no longer the heart of the home; it has been supplanted by the TV set. The programs on television may well be shaping the thoughts and ideas of future generations.

It is within this framework, therefore, that any local television station must operate. Challenges come on several fronts. Harmonious relationships must be maintained with the community, with the television and broadcasting industry at large, and with the Government of the United States as the licensor of the station which must always operate in the "public interest, necessity, and convenience." In living up to these obligations, as a responsible broadcaster, the general manager of the station also has the challenge of running his own operation at a profit—for the board of directors, stockholders, or owners to whom the general manager reports hold him, above all, responsible for sound business management.

THE GENERAL MANAGER'S RESPONSIBILITIES

It has been said that the station manager must be part educator and editor; psychologist, public relations man, and sociologist; businessman, lawyer, and engineer; and showman, to say the least. He must know and like people, and possess the quality of getting people to like and work with and for him. He must spend money wisely while being acutely conscious of costs. He should know selling as related to television specifically and the communications field generally. And he must always generate enthusiasm about the television broadcasting industry.

Basic planning and the direction of over-all station strategy are his chief responsibilities. The manner in which he performs these functions will be largely determined by the corporate structure of his station ownership group and the latitude permitted the general manager in running his operation. Ownership of television stations in the United States varies from that of individual ownership of a single station to multiple ownership and group operations

—representing people from diverse backgrounds, although newspaper, radio, and theater interests are predominant. The Federal Communications Commission, which grants television broadcasting licenses, has regulated station ownership to permit control of no more than five very high frequency (VHF) stations and two ultra high frequency (UHF) stations by one individual or stockholder group. Each of the three television networks—ABC, CBS, and NBC—is also allowed to own and operate television stations (in the number permitted by the FCC regulations) in addition to their over-all network operation. Consequently, each network owns and operates stations in major markets of the United States— referred to in the trade as "o-and-o" stations—the revenue of which contributes substantially to the financial strength of the networks. Other companies owning several stations include the Westinghouse Group, Storer Broadcasting, the Corinthian Group, and the Time-Life Stations, among others.

Policy may differ among the large group ownership organizations and the networks concerning the functions of the general manager of their individual stations. In the network operations, the general manager usually also holds the position of vice president, and reports directly to the vice president (or president) in charge of the owned-and-operated stations. In a group-owned station the general manager may report to the vice president in charge of the group. For greater flexibility, some companies permit the general manager complete autonomy of direction at the local level. In larger operations, there is usually a station manager who is directly responsible for the supervision of the individual station under the direction of the general manager.

Under the smaller station ownership, the general manager sometimes may also be a vice president and officer of the corporation, and very often serves in actual capacity as the station manager. Obviously, the more affluent stations in the major markets are in a position to employ more personnel and with more specialization than do the smaller market stations; many in the top major markets have hundreds of people on their payrolls which, of course, permits considerable diversification of programming and wider scope of community services. The revenue, the size of the market, and the complexity of station programming determine the scope of the staff and the number of aids available to the general

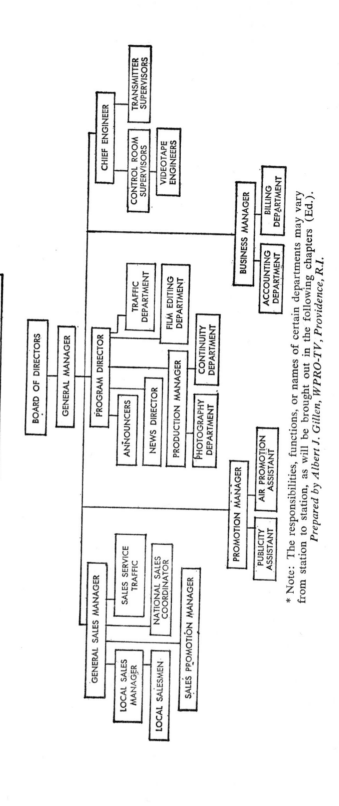

**TABLE OF ORGANIZATION
OF A TYPICAL TELEVISION STATION***

BOARD OF DIRECTORS

GENERAL MANAGER

CHIEF ENGINEER

CONTROL ROOM SUPERVISORS

TRANSMITTER SUPERVISORS

VIDEOTAPE ENGINEERS

PROGRAM DIRECTOR

TRAFFIC DEPARTMENT

FILM EDITING DEPARTMENT

ANNOUNCERS

NEWS DIRECTOR

PRODUCTION MANAGER

CONTINUITY DEPARTMENT

PHOTOGRAPHY DEPARTMENT

BUSINESS MANAGER

ACCOUNTING DEPARTMENT

BILLING DEPARTMENT

PROMOTION MANAGER

PUBLICITY ASSISTANT

AIR PROMOTION ASSISTANT

GENERAL SALES MANAGER

SALES SERVICE TRAFFIC

NATIONAL SALES COORDINATOR

LOCAL SALES MANAGER

LOCAL SALESMEN

SALES PROMOTION MANAGER

* Note: The responsibilities, functions, or names of certain departments may vary from station to station, as will be brought out in the following chapters (Ed.).
Prepared by Albert I. Gillen, WPRO-TV, Providence, R.I.

manager to relieve him of day-to-day management detail. (See accompanying table of organization—Ed.)

Major market stations also call upon specialized personnel to supervise labor relations, legal matters, business management and purchasing. To the small operation, however, these are "luxury specialists"—desirable but not usually employed on a permanent staff basis because of economic restrictions.

Network Relationships

A network enters into an affiliation agreement with the individual station licensee to be the outlet in that particular marketing area for the network's programming. The term "marketing area," rather than the specific city of license, is used because the television signal cuts across arbitrary city or county boundary lines and very often embraces a sizable number of counties. It may follow that one or more important cities within that area may then take on a hyphenated market identification, larger in size and importance than any single city in the market.

The contractual agreement with the network is generally for a period of two years and is renewable for successive two-year periods unless cancelled upon notice by either party. Once the formal affiliation begins, the general manager becomes the liaison between his station and the network in all subsequent negotiations between these two interdependent parties—the network as the programming and selling source, and the station as the advertising outlet in the market. Under this framework, the network assigns a member of its Station Relations staff to work with the station on such matters as network compensation, program clearances, rights and co-operative changes. The general manager attends joint network-affiliate meetings, gets briefed on network policy and program changes, and works for close rapport.

Programming

The essence of television as a business operation is the diversity of its programming. The viewing public expects to see—and does see—news as it happens, public affairs and documentaries, sports spectacles and agricultural programs, government in action and political debates, education and religion, talk and discussion, music and variety, motion pictures and live drama, space shoots, comedy, and commercials.

The direction of programming with its many ramifications is a highly specialized field. The general manager of any television station does not himself determine all of the programming of his individual station, but he does exercise an important influence in shaping program policies. He relies on programming from his network, from the film and videotape shows that he may buy independently, and from the live programs his station produces locally for his individual community.

The costs of programming for television are continually rising —some say they are exorbitant—and these costs are a prime determinant for the general manager in deciding how to program his station. In most instances the general manager buys the film— syndicated and features—for his station, usually in conjunction with his sales manager and program director. The general manager must be well versed on the quality of film, on its saleability for his market, and on the bargaining techniques needed in the buying process. Film buying is an area where mistakes can prove costly as it is a major part of programming expenses. The network-affiliated station is able to rely considerably on the programming supplied by his network, but an independent station must place far greater emphasis on the use of film for program material and for sales revenue. (This is discussed in greater detail in the following chapter—Ed.)

By virtue of its network affiliation, the station is assured of a complete line-up of network programming, both commercial and sustaining. It hopes to gain considerable audience and sell valuable commercial announcements adjacent to such network programs. The many hours of programming available to a network-affiliate may be indicated by this example of the time periods a NBC affiliated station in the central time zone will have programmed for it daily by that network: It may carry programs from 7:00 AM to 12:00 noon, from 1:00 PM to 4:00 PM, from 5:30 to 6:00 PM (or 6:00 to 6:30 PM), from 6:30 PM to 10:00 PM, and from 10:15 PM (or 10:30) to 12:00 midnight. The wide variety of programs available on a daily basis are supplemented by the network with news specials, documentaries, sports classics of every category, and major special attractions ranging from live Presidential press conferences to historic man-in-space coverage.

It should be noted that not every station affiliated with a network receives commercial orders from all of the network's advertisers, requesting that the station be used to televise the advertiser's message. Several years ago stations could not carry a network program unless such stations were ordered commercially by the network advertiser of that program. More recently the networks have made it possible, through program service plans, for their affiliates to carry the programs not commercially ordered by deleting the commercials and substituting the station announcement, usually sustaining. And today, most programs are available to stations on a network cooperative basis. Nevertheless, the affiliated station would usually prefer to be ordered by the network advertiser as a part of the basic line-up. And so toward this end the general manager may have to spend time selling his station to the agencies of the network advertiser, and in his local market to that advertiser's broker or distributor, all the way up the line to the sales and marketing divisions of the client. There also are so-called representative firms specializing in expanding market lists for their particular clients. Of course, the network Sales Departments and their Sales Service staffs continually work at such expansion of their network commercial line-ups, and the general manager often works with them to get his station added. When it is realized that more and more network sales are of a participating nature, and often for a limited line-up of stations, this phase becomes increasingly important to the smaller market station.

The programming of 14 hours a day of network productions, combined with the over-all national and regional promotion of the network to build audience interest in its line-up, is a valuable asset to the network-affiliated station. (See also Chapters 4 and 7 in this connection—Ed.) Network programs, costing as much as $100,000 or even $200,000 each to produce, will tend to attract maximum audiences, enhance the revenue potential of the station, and make it a more valuable property for its ownership.

In addition to benefitting from network programming around which to base its locally-produced schedule, the affiliated station also gains the advantage of the resources of the extensive news staffs of the network which provide global coverage and nationally renowned newscasters that add both prestige and scope to the station. Local news, public affairs, and editorializing (if the station has an editorial policy), can further enhance the station's prestige (see Chapter 10—Ed.).

Programming of these types, whether locally originated or network produced, must be offered 12 months a year. Unlike so many other businesses, production cannot be very well adjusted to conform to seasonal demands. Nevertheless, demand does change by season. The summer months present a real problem to most television stations in smaller markets, as then revenue is less than during the fall, winter, or spring. Yet often the station is faced with increasing rather than decreasing costs during the summer. The general manager is not in a position to cut his staff considerably, as is the manager of an educational station. Moreover, he is faced with heavy vacation periods that need to be filled, often necessitating additional staff members to be added as vacation replacements or increased overtime and increased work load on his existing staff. Furthermore, it is a time when he and his staff must finalize plans for fall changes in programming, and it is usually a hectic period.

Many station managers criticize the system that offers very little in new program ideas for summertime viewing. Management understands that film producers create 38 or 39 new films in a series so that 14 or 13 reruns may be used and production costs amortized over 52 weeks.* On the other hand, this film policy lends support to the caustic charges by newspaper competitors, and even by some local radio competitors, that nothing but reruns is programmed during the summertime. It is often felt that the problem is further exacerbated, not by the lack of creative personnel but by a lack of desire on the part of producers to create new program ideas that will bring fresh talent before the public on an experimental basis during the summer months. People do watch television during the summer, and would be willing to spend more time watching new programs that have a vitality that invites renewed interest and attention.

* Film production may even range to 34 new and 18 reruns over 52 weeks.

PERSONNEL AND PLANNING

Personnel matters occupy much of the general manager's time and attention. The best administrators are those with the ability to select, hire, and direct qualified personnel. The largest television stations employ a personnel manager to hire people for general and administrative jobs; and he, in turn, may delegate hiring of technical and program specialists to the respective department heads. The general manager, of course, has the prerogative of choosing his key people. He must make sure in this connection, that he surrounds himself with competent personnel who are experienced and knowledgeable about their specific departmental tasks, and are themselves fair and able administrators. Because the general manager spends so much time on community and industry activities, it becomes imperative that his key departmental personnel function not only autonomously within their own spheres of activity but also as a coordinated team within the framework of the over-all station operation. The general manager must work closely with his key people, must have their confidence and respect, must be able to delegate responsibility and authority for such responsibility to them.

The general manager will very likely call a planning meeting at least once each week, involving top station personnel and embracing strategy on all phases of the television station operation. Plans are formulated for sales and programming and promotion. Matters relating to internal control are reviewed, and station policies are implemented or changed. These meetings usually concern problem areas that require solution, and very often are heated "give and take" discussions that allow departmental personnel a voice in the operation. It is a healthy approach, and in this way the general manager gets a cross-section of opinion on certain phases of the operation with which he may not be totally familiar. During each week he will undoubtedly also meet with each department head individually and iron out problems for that individual that are outside the coordinated teamwork of the planning group. His conferences conceivably will range from discussions of editorials and news policy, to analyses of the need for a translator station or new construction on his site; from plans for television coverage of the State Fair to promotion ideas for the new season.

Bear in mind that the general manager is not an expert in every phase of the television operation. He serves primarily as an administrator and coordinator of a highly specialized team of experts. The intensity of the operation, and the constant pressures of working against time, may bring flaring of tempers and sharp disagreement on many operational matters. In such cases, it is the general manager who must make the final decisions in the best interests of the station.

Personnel cost control is essential. How to eliminate wasted man hours and consolidate work tasks is a constant challenge. The networks and large group operations periodically hire management consultant firms specializing in this field. Sometimes, as a result of their reports, we see periodic major shake-ups which may leave severe morale problems that have lasting effect upon job security. But it is most important that there be a constant search for more efficient operations through top quality performance. This can come about only through insistence upon improved selection of personnel, better scheduling of work assignments, closer supervision, improvement in equipment, orderly arrangement of the physical plant, and wider employee interest in the growth and development of the station.

LABOR RELATIONS

A large part of a television station's personnel will often be represented by one or more labor unions. When a labor union is certified by the National Labor Relations Board to be the official bargaining agent for any given unit of employees, the general manager must take the responsibility to carry on discussions with his own personnel and, in dealing with the union officials and the NLRB, to establish the nature of the bargaining unit and arrange for a proper election. The general manager becomes the prime representative of the station in formal negotiations with the union to effect an equitable contract. Wherever possible, he will hire competent legal counsel trained in labor law to advise and consult with him at all stages. Once the negotiations are concluded the general manager must devote close attention to the drawing up of the formal contract between the union and the company, set the agreement into writing, and disseminate its terms to each of the department heads involved.

Television stations in major markets are faced with more or less perpetual union problems as most big cities are highly organized, particularly in the entertainment field. It is not unlikely, in fact, that the general manager and his legal staff may deal with dozens of unions. The technical end of the business generally is represented by The International Brotherhood of Electrical Workers (IBEW) and The National Association of Broadcast Employees and Technicians (NABET), and in larger markets The International Alliance of Theatrical Stage Employees (IATSE) controls stage and production employees. Jurisdiction over announcers and talent is for the most part controlled by The American Federation of Television and Radio Artists (AFTRA) and by The Screen Actors Guild (SAG). These are a few of the major unions involved in television, although the number varies in accordance with the size of the station (down to perhaps one union in stations in smaller markets). On the other hand, many stations have no unionization of employees, and it is interesting that in recent years unions have made very few gains in the broadcasting field.

CONTROL OF OPERATIONS

Considerable time and attention must be devoted to close internal control of the operation. Television broadcasting is a business and must show a profit. The problems of profit and loss, income and expenses always wind up as the general manager's key responsibility, despite the fact he has sales managers and controllers and an accounting department to assist him in increasing revenue and controlling the costs of the operation. In short, he must have a thorough working knowledge of the financial aspects of his business. (See also Chapter 6 in this connection—Ed.)

One important means of internal control is the budget, the supervision and preparation of which must be guided by the general manager, who must also make sure that there is a constant check to compare budgeted expenses against the actual costs of operation. Indeed, any major difference in expenses from those budgeted for any specific period must be justified to ownership.

There must be a proper procedure to control cash receipts and disbursements—including the payroll. In many operations the general manager personally signs the payroll checks each week as this routine may bring to light deviations which call for investigation with the various department heads to determine possible correction. Overtime is one of the major items, and this entails discussions with the operations staff to re-schedule or re-program in order to cut it down.

In addition to his concern with sales, the general manager must also cross-check on collection of accounts receivable. This presents a real problem to television stations in many of the secondary and smaller markets, particularly where most time sales are made to the local businessman and not handled through advertising agencies. To a station that deals primarily in spot announcement business from national advertisers, receivables control, although important, is not the pressing matter that it is to the station dealing considerably in local time sales placed directly with the client. Many managers make it a daily ritual to have a receivables report on their desk the first thing each morning. This is a prerequisite to discussion with the local sales manager of the station to keep him posted on the status of delinquent accounts. The general manager must sometimes make the decision to take clients off the air, to turn over accounts for collection, and even to initiate legal suit for collection of certain accounts. In this respect he may, of course, find himself at variance with the local sales manager and sales staff. It is usually the general manager who must authorize write-offs of bad debts and approve credit on disputed accounts. In fact, it is a good policy for him to be the only source in the organization to do so, for generally the local sales manager and staff will be too lenient in dealing with local clients whom they must recontact for their livelihood.

In the control of purchases, the general manager must make sure that strict procedures are followed whereby each department head seeks out the lowest available prices for his purchases. He must see that there is a system of purchase orders and that needs of the departments are anticipated in advance so as to minimize last-minute rush orders. For the most part, the general manager will probably insist that the purchase orders come across his desk for inspection, or for signature and final approval before the purchase is authorized. Most stations will make their purchases within their own business community. The larger cities may offer wider selection and more opportunity for savings on purchases of many items of equipment and supply. However, this is not always the case in smaller cities, and the general manager must weigh the cost disadvantages of "purchasing locally" against the savings he may be able to effect by purchasing outside of his home city. There is an understandable sensitivity on the part of local business to keep the dollars within each community, and in this area the general manager at times may experience some conflict—to the extent that he may lose valuable local business if he authorizes purchases elsewhere. The over-all expenditures and payroll of the television station are, of course, important to the economy of the community. They help the station image throughout the area and often indirectly influence the sale of advertising for the station.

SALES

As a rule, the general manager wants to be informed about day-to-day sales developments. In many stations he personally directs sales, in consultation with his national and local sales managers. It is not unusual to find the general manager himself handling national sales, communicating with the various offices of the station's national sales representative throughout the country, and actually disseminating availabilities (commercial time available for sale) and confirming spot orders. Surveys show that many general managers have moved up into their positions through the sales field. So it is logical that they should continue to retain direct interest and some supervision in this important area of a station's operation.

PUBLIC RELATIONS

A community of viewers in any given city will include those who are always critical. They complain about summer repeats, and then complain when fall changes bring new programs to replace old favorites. Unfortunately, people with varied socio-economic backgrounds and having a wide diversity of interests expect a television station to provide each interest group with the type of programming that appeals specifically to it. They want better programming, more programming, different programming—and fewer commercials! Is not the station supposed to operate in the public interest, necessity and convenience? Some groups are extremely vocal; others are regrettably quiet. Criticism comes more frequently than praise, and criticism must be answered.

The problems in this area call for the public relations skill of the general manager. He has an important responsibility to act as the liaison between his station and the public; to bear the criticism and accept the compliments. He must be available to speak before innumerable groups in the community and answer intelligently all interrogations about his television operation; about the network with which his station is affiliated, and those networks with which he is not affiliated; about his station's news and editorial policies and its public affairs programming; about his station's over-all programming policies, and about his reasons for carrying or not carrying certain shows. The culture groups want more culture, and the mass audience wants less culture. He must be responsive to these community requests—and they are endless.

A resumé of his telephone calls each week would reveal that he answers viewer questions running the gamut of his program schedule from sign-on to sign-off; takes calls for tickets to network programs from people in his community who will visit New York and Hollywood; follows through on client requests for hard-to-get tickets to sports attractions; makes hotel reservations; explains why he cannot get passes to the theater; accepts or declines invitations to various functions in his community. It may be symbolic of his status that he is invited to share a place at the speaker's table and to participate in many important activities of his community, but finding time to attend the myriad meetings and functions becomes a real problem. Somewhere on his agenda he must make time to see his family and seek respite from the increasing pressures of daily television life.

Leaders of the community recognize the forceful role of the television station in public affairs, seek its aid on projects vital to the community, and call upon its key management personnel to help on programs in the public interest.* It is not unusual, therefore, to find the general manager on the board of directors of United Community Services, working with Junior Achievement, aiding the Symphony Orchestra Association, consulting with the Mental Health Society, soliciting funds for the Y.M.C.A. building campaign, directing public relations for the Public Library, and serving numerous health and welfare groups throughout the year.

The concomitant of this involvement is that the general man-

* For a comprehensive treatment of this subject, see *Television in the Public Interest* by A. William Bluem, John Cox and Gene McPherson, Hastings House, 1961.

ager must also actively seek out the opinions and solicit expressions of the community and its opinion leaders. He and his staff must work closely with religious, health and welfare, cultural, educational, agricultural, industrial, civic and governmental representatives and enable them to use station facilities and air time for public service.

In many cases, even though it would be more appropriate initially to delegate such contacts to others in his organization, from a public relations standpoint the general manager refrains from doing so. So we find numerous examples of his initiating public service programming on the station and then assigning its execution to the programming or public affairs departments. Not a day passes without the matter of public affairs taking some part of the manager's busy schedule.

At the risk of sounding trite, it can be said that the general manager devotes his personal services because he is truly dedicated to the philosophy of public service. Work with the community at large, and with specific community agencies and their leaders, brings its own rewards to him in the furtherance of worthy causes. It is deeply satisfying to know that the community approaches the television station and its manager as a prime source of assistance.

INDUSTRY RELATIONS

The general manager is not only involved in community affairs, but in industry relations as well. Television broadcasting is replete with various associations that require station participation and management activity. Foremost, of course, is the National Association of Broadcasters. During the year the general manager participates in NAB affairs and, of course, attends the annual NAB convention and possibly one or more of its regional conclaves. Frequently he takes advantage of the NAB expertise and source materials available to him from that Association in guiding his own station operation. The NAB provides him services on many fronts, and his contacts with the NAB for research and updated industry information are frequent.

On the state-wide level, the general manager affiliates with his state broadcasting association and takes an active role in its campaign not only to promote television broadcasting intrastate but also to serve as watchdog against harmful intrusions of broadcaster rights in the legislature. The general manager usually attends annual meetings of his state association, serves on one or more of its committees, and very likely is on immediate call for lobbying assistance at the capital city during sessions of the state legislature.

To help promote television generally as an advertising and sales medium, he takes membership in the TVB, the Television Bureau of Advertising, which works on the national level to acquaint advertisers throughout the nation with the advantages of television.

Not every manager spends time with national and state association business, which by some is looked upon with indifference and by others is set aside as a matter for concern of the professionals in the field. However, it would appear that only by concerted interest and participation on the part of top management in such activities can the television industry assert its strength and safeguard its security in the legislative halls.

The general manager necessarily turns with concern toward Washington and the regulations and policies of the Federal Communications Commission. Governmental regulation of the industry results in many pressing issues for the manager's deliberation and study. As a consequence, he must reflect carefully concerning how his station operation may be affected by such matters as proposals to limit the number of television commercials, the possibility of compulsory live local programming in certain blocks of prime time, conflicting policies relating to editorializing, as well as many other rules and regulations of the Commission.

Why does anyone want to manage a television station in the light of the many tribulations of an ever-changing industry? Is there some powerful redeeming factor to compensate for the pressures of always operating against the clock; the pressures by ownership for greater profit in the face of increasing costs; the pressures imposed by the community and its changing attitudes and tastes; and by the growing pressures of government and its regulatory practices? One hears few complaints by the general manager about his role in life: he earns a good income, holds prestige and status in his community, and enjoys his personal accomplishments and that of his television station.

More important, television broadcasting is deeply ingrained within him and has engulfed him with magnetic attraction. He has spent most of his adult years in the business, has risen through the ranks of television station operation, and "lives" television each hour of the day. He looks ahead and sees in television a volatile, fertile field whose potential is still untapped. Changing technical developments, the growth of color, the entry of space communications, experimental program concepts—all present a vibrant challenge to his faculties. Each broadcasting day brings different goals and new horizons to conquer, and the general manager does not want to miss one exciting opportunity to be part of the most fascinating business in the world.

CHAPTER 4

The Independent Station

BY RICHARD B. RAWLS

KPHO-TV, Phoenix, Arizona

One of the early pioneers in television, Mr. Rawls began his career with the Columbia Broadcasting System in 1939. He subsequently worked in virtually every phase of the broadcasting industry before joining the Meredith Broadcasting Company in 1952 as general manager of their radio and television stations in Phoenix, Arizona, where he is now Vice President of KPHO Radio and Television. Competing in a four-station market, Mr. Rawls has drawn nation-wide attention to his television station as one of the most successful and impressive independent operations in the country.

THE independent television station is one that is not affiliated with or owned by a national network. As of this writing, there are some 35 commercial independent stations; of these, three are located in New York City and four are in Los Angeles. Most of the other independents are located in four-station or five-station markets.

Both the independent and network affiliated station have approximately the same pattern of organizational structure, similar responsibilities to the community and to the Federal Communications Commission to maintain high standards of programming—whether locally originated or purchased as film or program package from outside sources. Both the independent and the affiliate have substantially the same kind of physical plant and equipment.

The total staff required to operate a medium-size station may vary from 40 to 60 persons. This is true of the independent as well as the affiliated station. The larger the staff, the more extensive the services of non-broadcasting personnel—promotion, accounting, engineering, secretarial, switchboard, mail room, janitorial, and other clerical help. The station with the smaller staff assigns many of these administrative duties among the pure broadcasting help— the sales manager shares the promotional duties; the programming and traffic people share the telephone and bookkeeping jobs; the operations engineer performs the necessary executive detail; and the secretarial staff is held to a minimum. All too often, however, the manager of the independent station will pattern his staff organization and operational practices after one of his competitors who operates the lush affiliated station. This type of management may be dictated by ownership; sometimes by pride; and, in some instances, it is dictated by a desire to "belong," to have equal status, even though the potential profit opportunity may make such an operation not at all practical. In any case, both the independent and the affiliated station in the same market operate with generally comparable staffs. Here the similarities end.

How the Independent Differs from the Affiliate

The independent must make its way alone, and this is fundamentally the independent's problem. The affiliated station receives from the network some 3,000 hours of free programming service each year, plus a substantial revenue given in return for carrying the network commercials. On the other hand, the independent pays all programming costs while lacking, too, the guarantee of network revenue. True, both the independent and affiliate each start the fiscal year alike—at zero dollars. However, before the independent throws the switch for the first day of broadcasting, its zero dollars become zero minus the cost of 3,000 hours of programming for that year and, additionally, minus the dollar amount that will be paid to the affiliate by its network—and such an amount could be about 30% of the affiliated station's gross revenue for the year; or putting it another way, an amount capable of paying as much as 50% of the annual operating overhead.

It is a difficult problem, but not insoluble. Some of the independent stations in the larger markets are doing very well; the shoe pinches the hardest for the independent in the medium to smaller markets where there are significantly less TV homes. What are the approaches to solving the problem? Basically, they include: 1) competent, informed management with television know-how; 2) carefully selected, experienced personnel with the right attitude; 3) a carefully worked-out plan of attack; 4) sufficient funds to pay for the starting load costs. These are some of the prerequisites. The goal itself is to produce, with a realistic budget, a reasonable share of the audience against network-affiliated competition. Only then can the independent be commercially strong locally and in the national marketplace.

THE GENERAL MANAGER AND THE PLAN OF ATTACK

Let us consider the role of the general manager in effecting this goal. The organizational structure, as has been noted, of an independent and an affiliated station in the same market are approximately the same in terms of personnel and their duties. There is only the difference in management emphasis. For the independent, there is no network association through which an operating philosophy can be established; there is no network guidance in the areas of programming, sales, promotion, engineering or research. So the general manager of the independent must start from scratch, as it were, in setting up the operating policy of his station.

Think of the independent as being a sort of "mama and papa store" competing against the big department store chain. The general manager of the independent station must be a well informed fellow; he must know what he is doing and he must understand the operations in each department. He should be a man of unending enthusiasm, prepared to cope with constant challenges, and who can communicate these traits to his staff.

But what is the independent station's plan of attack? Let us assume that we are in competition, in a hypothetical market, with three network affiliates. The first step is to watch these operations, and become as familiar as possible with them. Study their programming, particularly the program segments they *originate*. Are they being defeated in their local efforts because the programming they originated, or purchased, is not compatible with the adjacent network programming? Or are they enhancing the network programs and their own stations with careful choices of local programming?

Let us further assume that the stations in our market may be clearly ranked: first, second, third and fourth—the fourth being the independent. Pictorially, then, we have a saw-tooth chart that is something like a ski slope running down hill, from left to right. The first, or dominant station, is at the top of the hill (and by a dominant station is meant one that consistently has the largest share of audience). Such dominance may be achieved by "riding" the popular network, by promoting the network effectively and, above all, by doing a good job of leading in and out of network "feeds." (In some cases, particularly due to time-zone differences, a station may move network programs out of original "day and time" feed to more productive time periods so as further to assure dominance.) The station that ranks second or third in the ski slope chart might be riding the popular network but doing the job poorly, or it may be affiliated with a less popular network. As to the independent in fourth place, it may be doing a relatively good job if it is able to capture first or second place in audience share in certain of its program segments. The independent can be satisfied with fourth place, in fact, if that ranking delivers approximately the same percentage of audience as the three competing network affiliates. (See Chapter 12 on Research, in this connection—Ed.) If our saw-tooth chart can be made to show almost a straight line, then pictorially we represent four stations, each with a comparable share of the available audience. And in such case, our chart would then show the independent delivering audience at about the same cost-per-thousand as its network-affiliated competitors.

How do we level off that slope? Starting with the raw mechanics—although the operation of an independent is not quite as simple as that—we know that we want to reduce the high peak audience dominance of the first-ranking station. It must be understood, in this connection, that at any given time the total available audience for all four stations in the market is fairly static. The total of homes tuned to television does not change too much from day to day, or from month to month. Our share cannot be raised, or lowered, without it affecting the position of the other stations. Our technique, therefore, is to program strength against strength, to lower a peak—the intent, of course, being that our strength should lower the dominant peak by switching audience to us and thus raising our peak. There are times, however, when we do not have additional strong programming to expend, or we may not have available the type of programming that could be productive in a certain time period. In such case, we may then program weakness against strength to help raise one of the peaks of a different competing station. Or, we may program weakness against weakness in an effort to let still another competitor get a new lead. In short, this becomes a sort of "cat and mouse" game. There are, of course, other tricks such as planning lead-in and lead-out programming to carry over or to retain our audience, or the device of placing a dramatic hour program across competitive half-hours. Even though these and other such techniques are best suited to a skilled program director, the general manager must understand these practices (see Chapter 7—Ed.).

FILM BUYING

It will be recalled that the independent needs to produce or procure the 3,000 hours of programming per year which the affiliated station receives from the network. As a point of reference, let us stipulate that the programming of an independent station is 80% film. Therefore, the independent must buy sufficient film to fill 80% of 3,000 hours, or 2,400 hours of programming. Each month, then, will require 200 hours of film programming plus 50 hours of live studio, or remote, productions. And let's not forget that this is only the equivalent of the amount of programming that the network affiliate gets free. In view of the fact that the independent is operating 14 hours a day, or about 422 hours per month, an additional 172 hours of programming per month is needed to fill out the schedule—but this same 172 hours must also be produced or bought by the network affiliate. The independent station will probably program 80% of these hours with film, or 138 hours per month of additional film productions.

Some managers of independent stations assign to program directors, or film directors, the chore of buying film. Inasmuch as it represents so great an expense, film buying should be the business of the general manager. Remember, we are talking about an annual cost for film which could very well equal one-third of the total cost of operating the independent station.

To buy film for television is an exhilarating experience. The film distributors' representatives are a fine group of men. Of course, one has to be patient on occasion inasmuch as they have been trained to think in terms of tens of thousands of dollars—yes, even in hundreds of thousands of dollars. In dealing with them the best advice to remember is that 100-cent dollars are being spent, and they are hard dollars to come by. Keep in mind that, when $100,000 is spent on film, almost $1,000,000 worth of telivision time and talent must be sold by the station to get that $100,000 back and show a profit!

To get down to cases, when buying film everybody knows that the independent's major programming must be film. Naturally, the dominant station in the market wants to stay dominant; therefore, it is the logical prospect for the best film available because it will pay the best prices. Also remember, the other ranking stations share the independent's enthusiasm for becoming dominant, or at least more saleable, and they too will bid high. In this situation, the independent has to make haste slowly. There is the trick of bidding the prices up, and getting a station in the middle. Don't let them do it; just stand firm. It is also possible that a competitor will buy more good film than he needs, just to keep it "off the market." If so, he will spend budget for film he really does not need for important programming because he fears this film might have been programmed against his strong audience segments, and thus might have lowered his audience share. Let him corner the film market, and then film can be bought at prices more compatible with requirements. Anything that can be done to help competitors, all of them, become fully supplied with film may make a four-station market into a one- or two-station market as far as film buying is concerned. The prices are always high in a market of four or more stations, as film seems to be priced at what the traffic will bear. If the supply is limited and the demand is strong, prices are high but, if there are fewer buyers, the prices are lower.

There is no little man sitting in an ivory tower somewhere setting film prices, because if there were, there would be some consistency to the price structure. There is none, so don't try to rationalize the offering prices. Above all, if a film product is wanted, make a firm offer. It is best not to discuss a film property at all if one has no need for it. Establish the need, offer a price (regardless of the asking price), and stand firm! The film may be lost to a competitor, but the next "buy" can probably be picked up.

LIVE PROGRAMMING

All television stations, whether network affiliates or independent, must do a certain amount of live programming if they are to serve their market properly. The number of hours of locally originated programming varies, but the independent will probably produce a minimum of 85 hours per month. Of these, some are studio shows and a few are remote productions. The only thing to emphasize here is that the independent should try to do these programs better than do the affiliated stations. I know of an independent that held first place in audience in news and children's programs for years. It can be done.

COSTS OF OPERATION

Let us look, in a general way, at the cost of operating a television station of medium size. There is an old rule of thumb for judging the approximate total operating cost, not as applicable today as it once was but it will serve our purpose. First count the personnel— let us assume, in this case, 50 people. Multiply the number of persons by $1,000 to arrive at the total operating cost per month —$50,000. Thus, the total for the year may be estimated as $600,000.

Such a figure, for total annual cost of operation, may be applied either to an affiliated station or an independent. However, it must be remembered that the independent must provide 3,000 hours of programming which, as mentioned earlier, could be equivalent to 50% of the affiliated station's total operating cost—or, in this case, $300,000. Add this cost of programming to the estimated $600,000 in our formula above, and we arrive at $900,000 as the independent's total cost of operation for the year.

It would serve no particular purpose to attempt to estimate revenue for a typical independent as revenue figures vary with the size of the market. A limitation applying to all independents, however, is the fact that the profit potential is greatly restricted by the absence of network programs that attract national and local business, and by the absence of guaranteed income from a network ($300,000, in the example given above).

PERSONNEL: PLANNING AND TRAINING

It is important to have qualified personnel, people with good experience and eager for the challenges of an independent's operation (and this should be made clear at the outset). If there is a choice between two people with approximately equal experience, the one with the right attitude ought to be picked. In many television stations, there are too many "Chiefs" and too few "Indians," and this sort of thing should be avoided. The general manager should select his department heads wisely, limiting the number to a group that can get the job done.

No matter how comprehensive the general manager's experience may have been, he cannot manage a station alone, nor can it be managed properly in a dictatorial manner. It is therefore desirable to set up a management board, a method of operation that is applicable to the network affiliated station as well as to the independent.

A well-rounded management board selection would include the general manager, as chairman, and the following department heads as members: station manager, sales manager, program director, chief engineer, office manager, promotion manager. Should the name "management board" conflict with a particular organizational set-up, then another name may be chosen such as: planning board, executive committee, station board, or any other suitable name which is indicative of the work to be performed. The group should be scheduled to meet as often as may be required; in the beginning it may be necessary to meet once or twice a week but in a very short time these meetings may be reduced to every two weeks, and eventually to once each three months. Before calling the meeting, suggestions should be requested from the members for items to be discussed. Written agenda should be prepared and circulated to them in advance. The purpose of these meetings is to discuss future planning and improve communication among staff members on such matters as: station policies, the attitude of the station in the community, the public service aspects, the sales aspects, general programming policies, responsibility to the Federal Communications Commission, personnel policies, technical facilities, and promotional plans. It is most important to have a good recording secretary to take minutes, which should be circulated soon after each meeting. The secretary should be most careful to record projects to be performed or started before the next meeting—and the names of those responsible for the respective jobs.

The work of the management board will motivate department head meetings, and these should be encouraged to be held as often as necessary. Of course, meetings such as these are time-consuming, and while the management meetings are best when scheduled at the end of the day, the department meetings usually bring best results when they are held at the beginning of the day.

The projects developed in the various meetings must be followed up and pushed through to a successful conclusion. It is well to invent some mechanical means to assure completion of these items. The best way to accomplish this is a system of mimeographed paper forms. Each set of forms should be designed to itemize each element of a given project and to indicate when it has been resolved. Provide sufficient copies for routing, and if necessary for emphasis, resort to colored mimeo stock. A small box on each form giving directions for its use and flow-information will speed up the work. Institute as many forms as are deemed necessary. The system will not only improve communication among members of the staff, but will be a valuable aid in training people to do their particular part of the project efficiently.

Among the 50 persons on the staff, there are probably only seven sales personnel: the station manager, the sales manager, four salesmen—and the general manager. The other 43 persons are not revenue producers; to the contrary, they are cost items and they are there to service the salesmen. This is one important point which must be put across to all staff members: they are there to manufacture the product the salesman sells and they must do this efficiently; they are there to service the salesmen and deliver the product as promised. Without the salesman, there is no need for the rest of the staff.

PUBLIC RELATIONS

The general manager of a television station will automatically receive the attention of the community it serves. This dignified position must be earned through tangible work in every civic effort. The general manager will be called on many times to contribute time and skills, and in many instances, the skills of his staff. This responsibility should be accepted enthusiastically, so that the station will enjoy the respect of the community.

Continuing emphasis must be placed on being thoroughly familiar with the market. A great deal of research material is available from local organizations which they will be glad to share upon request. When the station manager makes sales trips to the larger cities to meet with his national sales representatives, he is the one who must be well informed and fluent on this particular subject—a one-man Chamber of Commerce, in fact. Particularly in the medium-to-smaller areas which do not rank among the first 50 markets in TV homes, the most important selling job of a station is to get its market on the advertisers' buying list. It is not until then that there will be an opportunity to sell the station nationally.

The general manager must participate in trade associations and must make it a point to take advantage of all of the valuable material which will be afforded. In smaller TV operations where there is little money to support lawyers, professional engineers, and other professional advice, these association materials and services are of the greatest help to management. The leading national organizations, such as the National Association of Broadcasters and the Television Bureau of Advertising, should not have to seek the station out for membership. On the local level there is no limit to the opportunities to join trade associations, most of which are allied to the station's interests, including: the local broadcasting group, the downtown merchants, the Grocers State Association, the Electric League, and many others.

BUDGETING

The general manager will be expected to produce, in advance, an estimate of budget expectations for the year ahead, and this is a high priority call on his skill and his time. It is desirable to have the privilege of review and amendment at the end of each quarter. Projections must be compared with the station's performance as frequently as the office manager or accountant can get to the job. An effective way to watch progress is to require a report of gross dollar sales as often as every day if possible. Performance records, once established, will greatly simplify the budgeting problem for ensuing years.

It is desirable, in fact, to draw up a five-year plan. This will be a budget of sorts, but primarily it will be an estimate of the goal expressed in total gross and net figures. The format of the estimate must be very comprehensive so as to reflect such factors as: economic trends, growth or deterioration of the market, changes in population, normal increases or decreases in costs, expansion of services, the acquisition of new property and equipment, increases in payroll due to merit, or cutbacks permitted through increased efficiency. Increases in rate schedules should be projected, as well as increases in costs due to the growth of revenue requiring additional expenses for services and outside consultation. In short, the budget format should fit future plans for growth. Many of the market projection figures needed for this will be available from such sources as local banks and utility companies, the national trade associations, and the television research services. Revenue figures for past performance or in markets of similar size, may be readily obtained from the Federal Communications Commission. Such a study will prove to be one of the general manager's most stimulating, informative and gratifying personal projects.

CHAPTER 5

The Educational Television Station

BY GEORGE A. BAKER

WETA-TV, Washington, D. C.

After graduating from Amherst College, Mr. Baker began his radio-television career in Buffalo, New York, in 1934 and ten years later joined NBC-Radio as a producer-director, moving into television in Washington after the war. When medical color-television was installed at Walter Reed Hospital in Washington in 1956, he became Executive Producer and the following year was named by the National Academy of Sciences to the U.S. Committee for the International Geophysical Year. During this assignment he also acted as television advisor to the Greater Washington Educational Television Association. In 1961, Mr. Baker became General Manager of the newly-licensed educational station, WETA-TV, in Washington, D.C. On January 1, 1964 he resigned to accept a Special Projects position at the White House in Washington.

THE philosophy of the educational broadcaster is significantly different from that of his commercial colleagues. While the latter have the responsibility of operating their stations in "the public interest, convenience, and necessity," they also have the privilege of making a profit by selling time on the air. To make this profit, the majority of their programs are designed primarily for entertainment. The greater the entertainment value, the larger the audience, and the greater the selling power of the program. The program becomes a means to an end. But for the educational broadcaster, the program is the end product, designed to enrich, uplift and/or inform. The educational station strives to serve the complex interests of the community on a continuing basis, with responsibility but without economic pressures, for the benefit of the total audience or any minority segment.

Educational television stations generally are owned by a university, a school district, a state, or a community. A university-owned station began the educational television movement in 1953 when the Board of Regents of the University of Houston authorized KUHT. School districts, too, soon learned the value of television, as in the case of KRMA in Denver, a station licensed to School District #1 of the City and County of Denver, and which is owned and supported by the public school system. State-owned stations are growing in number also, a heartening indication of state legislatures recognizing the value of ETV. The State of Alabama, for example, owns and operates four educational television stations which are interconnected in a micro-wave network and licensed to the Alabama Educational Television Commission. Similarly, there has been a proliferation of community-owned stations, beginning with WQED in Pittsburgh, owned by Metropolitan Pittsburgh Educational Television, a non-profit community organization of individuals interested in television to satisfy the special interests of the community.

Like the commercial station, an educational station is concerned with two broad areas: its financial condition and the nature of its programming. Let us first consider the matter of solvency, without which there can be no television, good, bad or indifferent.

LEGAL LIMITATIONS OF ETV

An educational station is, of course, non-commercial. The Federal Communications Commission rule on consideration, Section 3.621 (d) reads:

> "An educational station may not broadcast programs for which a consideration is received, except programs produced by or at the expense of or furnished by others than the licensee for which no other consideration than the furnishing of the program is received by the licensee. The payment of line charges by another station or network shall not be considered as being prohibited by this paragraph."

Of interest also in this connection is Section 3.621 (e) which states that the sponsor identification rules apply "to the extent applicable," with the proviso that: ". . . no announcements (visual or aural) promoting the sale of a product or service shall be transmitted in connection with any program." There is ambiguity in this regulation, but there is also flexibility. We suspect the ambiguity is deliberate, because it would be a virtual impossibility to spell out every circumstance which might require special consideration. The intent of the rule is plain, however: under no circumstances can an educational station sell time on the air for the broadcast of any programs in the special interest of any person, product or service. This is a fundamental consideration by the FCC in granting an educational station license, and is one of the basic regulatory differences between commercial and educational operations.

While the FCC requires that any applicant for an ETV license must have non-profit status, "non-profit" does not mean that such a station cannot realize a surplus of income over expenditures. But such a surplus must not revert to any person or groups of persons as financial gain. It can be accrued as a reserve fund, used in expansion or for capital assets, donated to another non-profit use or even used as legitimate salary increases for personnel. Unfortunately, however, the dispensation of surplus is not a frequent problem in educational television.

SOURCES OF REVENUE AND SUPPORT

There are some basic sources of revenue, nevertheless, which are common to the four types of educational stations. First of all, there are the foundation grants which generally have been the cornerstone for capital funds. For the school district, university, and state-owned stations there have been tax funds and grants from educational institutions, and these have been provided for community stations as well to support in-school and adult education programming. Another source of income for ETV stations exists in the area of the production of programs for other stations or for various types of organizations. There are also federal contracts from the U. S. Department of Health, Education and Welfare available for the purchase of transmission facilities as a result of the Educational Television Facilities Act.

This legislation is a tremendous forward step in the progress of ETV, though frequently misinterpreted by the viewing public. (Some have even drawn the conclusion that educational television's money worries are over—it is going to be comfortably supported by government!) The government is offering support to both new and existing stations in helping them to buy certain expensive pieces of equipment on a matching funds basis. The equipment items are carefully stipulated; in general, they only include: camera chains, videotape recorders, switchers, transmission apparatus and antennae, with related installation gear. Not included are: ancillary studio items (lights, projectors, rear screen projection equipment, etc.), truck bodies for mobile units, buildings, or any of the extras that many stations need to add to their basic equipment for more sophisticated productions. Both the existing station, wishing to add to its facilities, and the new station, faced with the overwhelming cost of transmission equipment, must furnish supporting evidence to prove financial stability and capacity to match the proffered Federal funds, and justify their use of the facilities applied for.

Grants from other government agencies such as The National Science Foundation, and the National Aeronautics and Space Administration, often exclude the purchase of equipment, but may cover a wide variety of other project expenses such as consultant fees, overhead and rental of unusual or sophisticated devices. It is a sine qua non for any new ETV manager to become thoroughly familiar with the functions of these agencies and to study the types of proposals which have been of interest to them in the past. They are able to deal easily with non-profit, non-commercial stations and their wide-ranging roles make them an excellent possibility for some of ETV's more esoteric proposals. In this connection, it is well to note here that a large part of a manager's time is devoted to the conception and documentation of proposals for programs, surveys and special studies. Familiarizing himself with all types of proposal formats is an important part of the manager's job in ETV.

Gifts to the station may come from a variety of other sources and assume unusual forms: interest from endowment funds, bequests in wills, gifts of buildings, equipment or funds from friendly commercial stations, and a host of other sources of public support.

Some community stations actively involve the viewing public in money-raising by running membership campaigns. Others have established efficient door-to-door solicitations which seek contributions of any amount. Still another device is the benefit, and these run the gamut of ingenuity, including such things as: telethons, ten-dollar-a-plate-dinners, auctions, dances, picnics—all of these and more have brought in money for the continuance of operations.

Perhaps this review of the sources of support of educational television may suggest greater similarities than differences between the commercial manager and the educational manager. Both are actively engaged in the pursuit of revenue. The commercial manager strives for income from advertisers, as he works to increase profits. The ETV manager elicits monies from foundations, the government, and the community as he seeks to remain solvent.

PROGRAMMING

Like the commercial manager, the ETV manager is also deeply involved with his product, the programming of his station. The major distinction, of course, is that the ETV manager does not have the pressing need for maximum audience. The school district, university, and state-owned stations will concentrate primarily on in-school instruction. The community station will strive to serve the varied interests of its viewers. Some community stations will combine these functions. In so doing, some stations will insist on a great degree of autonomy in producing classroom programs, while others will feel just as strongly that they are merely a vehicle, and will leave all the elements of responsibility to the schools they serve.

WETA-TV in Washington, D. C. is an example of a middle-ground solution which has proved very flexible and has worked out to everyone's satisfaction. WETA's signal serves 17 school districts in nearby Maryland and Virginia. To meet all the requirements and effectively solve all the problems of so many school systems was quite obviously a major undertaking. To handle it a Curriculum Council was formed which was made up of representatives from each district. Sub-committees on programs, finance, etc., were drawn from this Council to meet and deal with such specialized problems. At the Council level, decisions were reached on which of the primary and elementary grades would be best served by television, which subjects should be televised, whether they would be direct instruction or enrichment programs, and the hour of broad-cast which would accommodate the greatest number of classrooms. From these recommendations on subject matter the Program Committee established the actual content of each program in science, language arts, music and other subjects as a guide for both the television teacher and the classroom teacher who would be expected to coordinate their efforts to extract the maximum of effectiveness from each lesson. Teachers from all the school systems were invited to apply for the job of television teacher, stating their qualifications just as they would have if they were entering a new teaching position. The applicants were culled on the basis of aptitude and, after individual interviews with the Council, several were chosen for an audition. At this point, for the first time, a representative of the program staff of WETA-TV entered the picture to adjudge the ability of the teachers to communicate effectively in the television medium. The final choice was made, and the successful applicant was then charged with the responsibility of making up a detailed guide or outline of program content for the school year. This guide serves as a manual for the classroom teacher who arranges her teaching schedule to coincide with the in-school lesson.*

This method of working gives the schools complete control over both contextual matters and teachers, leaving the station's producer free to join with the teacher in transforming the day's lesson into an instructional program that is both captivating and effectual. Maintaining a proper liaison between the Council and the station is the job of the In-School Coordinator on the WETA staff, who handles the multitude of details, attends Council and committee meetings, and reports to management and the school representatives. It is the happiest dichotomy imaginable, and works to the benefit of both the schools and the station.

ETV GOVERNING BODIES

The general manager of an Educational Television station operates as the representative of a governing body that establishes policy and renders administrative decisions. Such a body may be known as the State ETV Commission, the Board of Regents, the School

* *Teach With Television: A Guide to Instructional TV* by Lawrence Costello and George N. Gordon, Hastings House, 1961, offers a complete treatment of this subject.

Board, the Board of Trustees, or some comparable title depending most of all on the nature of the station itself. Such an overseeing group may seem inhibiting to a manager of a commercial station who may be less accustomed to group management. However, such a group of advisors can be an effective and responsive sounding board of highly intelligent and sensitive people. Their shrewd guidance in legal, business and financial matters is undoubtedly responsible for the record of success achieved by many stations.

There are varying degrees of control exerted by these governing bodies, since the function of the Board for each type of station must necessarily differ. In general, however, an empathy between Board and management which allows normal flexibility of action at the operations level is the most effective relationship. In the case of community stations, where the Board is representative of dedicated leaders in every aspect of community life, there is no question but that it can be the greatest single asset on the balance sheet.

NEED FOR TRAINED MANAGEMENT PERSONNEL

The Board has the responsibility for choosing the manager of the station. Presuming a good educational background and sufficient administrative experience, there are noticeable variants in the television training and background of management in the different classifications of stations. Where the operation is devoted entirely, or almost entirely, to meeting academic programming needs of an in-classroom variety, management may be charged to school administrative personnel or faculty members, since the station is actually a function of the school. As the scope of the station broadens and the commitment to community programming grows in volume, so does the need for solid television know-how in management. In a community station, the general manager or station manager often may be operating with a small staff and budget to match. This may not permit him the luxury of hiring a trained program manager or business manager or operations manager—posts which normally would be filled by men with strong, practical television backgrounds. The immediate solution lies in the manager assuming temporary responsibility for these necessary functions. It is not a good solution, but it is expedient. Only a manager with the expertise of solid operating experience could hope to function at all in these highly specialized jobs. It is also axiomatic that, in the competitive atmosphere of any multi-station market with its interplay among all stations, the general manager needs the "savvy" to meet his commercial counterparts on common ground, or risk the loss of station prestige brought on by his own inadequacies in the medium.

There is also the matter of experience necessary in the other top operating personnel of the station. The technical competence of the engineering people must be assumed, but programming or production competence must not be taken for granted. ETV has too many opportunities, mandates and responsibilities to risk putting its most sensitive and creative jobs in the hands of those who are not fully trained and qualified to hold them. Neither commercial nor academic training is enough in itself. The manager must look for that electric quality that is so needed to lift educational programming above the pedestrian level. As in all television programs, the viewer must be attracted to educational programming by inventive production if the medium is to achieve its goal of an informed public.

The need for trained, creative individuals becomes quite apparent when one considers some of the recondite source material that is often the base on which the program manager, producer and director must build. The educator may translate and communicate but the production people, in turn, must be able to modify or intensify their communication skills to make full use of the medium. In civic programming, the ETV producer is often faced with the job of preparing a palatable presentation from some indigestible components, and with a minimum of technical equipment. In order to avoid the label of mediocrity in his productions an ETV producer must call on all his ingenuity to overcome the problems of non-professional community talent, lack of available rehearsal time and space, shortage of facilities and limited budgets for graphics, sets and other materials. This takes skill, the kind of skill that is only at the command of an experienced practitioner in the TV arts. Such people are in demand and can pretty well control their market value, which normally would price them out of range of an ETV staff salary. But educational programming has something to offer them that is often more tempting than the higher income held out by standard stations. Fortunately such people are also artists, and many are intrigued by the variety, freedom and volume of ETV productions. All other qualifications being equal, the addition of even one such person to a staff will act as a catalyst for the entire operation.

To attract an audience, people must know the program is on the air, and this of course calls for promotion which, in the case of ETV, is largely a measure of ingenuity. It pays to advertise, but it also costs to advertise. Thus it is not surprising that, in educational television, the promotion manager works harder to get free publicity in the papers and program guides than does his commercial counterpart. Throughout the struggle, however, the press has exhibited a benign attitude toward this precocious infant, ETV, and has been an important help.

These, then, are the responsibilities of the general manager: to keep his station solvent, to program to the needs of the community, and to administer a staff that can be creative on a limited budget. But he does receive assistance from the several educational television organizations that render special services.

ETV SERVICE ORGANIZATIONS

The oldest of such agencies is the National Association of Educational Broadcasters (NAEB) with a large membership of institutions, organizations and individuals who are actively interested in educational broadcasting. NAEB publishes a great amount of valuable material in its *Journal, Newsletter* and Washington *Report*. It also provides legal and management consulting services and a placement service for both radio and TV personnel, and conducts seminars and conventions for informational exchange.

The Joint Council on Educational Broadcasting (JCEB) acts in the capacity of a legislative spokesman for the educational broadcasters. It has a council of top-ranking educators who recommend policy action to Federal regulatory agencies or to Congress.

The National Educational Television Center (NET, or Center) is a programming service agency with its main offices in New York City. Its primary function is that of a central programming agency for its affiliates across the country, and in this capacity it operates somewhat as a huge mail-order program network. For an extremely low annual affiliation fee it distributes by air express or parcel post programming in the categories of public affairs, science, humanities and fine arts, and children's programs. These are

produced by the Center and its affiliates on film, videotape or kine-
scope recording and represent the cream of national and international production efforts.

With the help of the ETV organizations, with the guidance of
the station's supervisory board, and with the support of his staff,
the general manager of an educational television station seeks to
actively involve himself in his community. His prime mission is
to serve the sensitive, inquisitive, and grateful viewers who look to
ETV to serve their special interests. The audience size may be
small, but this has the not inconsiderable advantage of bringing
the station into intimate contact with its viewers. The small number
of personnel at the station itself brings the general manager into
closer touch with his staff and helps build a spirit of *camaraderie,*
a feeling of pride in the station and its product. The final test for
the general manager is whether he has been able through his
work to earn the respect and confidence of his staff, the business
community, and viewers of educational television.

CHAPTER 6

The Controller's Role in Management

BY JOSEPH K. MIKITA

Group W, Westinghouse Broadcasting Company, New York

Now Vice President, Finance, of Westinghouse Broadcasting Company, Mr. Mikita has had a broad background in finance and administration. A native of Virginia, he graduated from Fordham University and then took his Master's degree from Columbia University. Following World War II, he was associated with S. D. Leidesdorft & Co., Certified Public Accountants, and subsequently Capital Cities Broadcasting Company. Mr. Mikita joined Westinghouse Broadcasting Company as Controller in 1958 and was elected to his present position two years later. He is on the Executive Committee of the Institute of Broadcasting Financial Management, and is a member of numerous professional associations.

THE medium of television as we know it today has been with us for over 15 years. The business of television, however, is just shedding its swaddling clothes. In its inception during the late 1940's and early 1950's, the television medium was absorbed with technical problems and the need to achieve audience levels high enough to give the industry stature as an advertising medium. Engineering, though always important, was particularly so in these early days and the need for producing equipment capable of disseminating a good signal over wide areas received considerable attention. More efficient transmitters, cameras, projectors and antennae had to be designed and built. Towers climbed higher into the sky, again to allow the signal to be transmitted over a broader area. Transmission lines were improved to reduce transmission loss and thereby increase the effectiveness of the signal being radiated.

This emphasis on "hardware" and people necessary to design, build and operate the equipment was an important factor in the rapid growth of television.

Similarly, and not too much later, "creativity" became a by-word and a great need for creating programming to satisfy the appetite of this young but voracious industry became a paramount consideration.

Here was a new medium which could bring sight and sound directly into the homes of people—a medium that was literally begging for something new which would entertain and inform the masses. Here was a tremendous opportunity for creative people to provide a product sorely needed and which had limited opportunity for exposure in the past. Live shows were the thing and, as show-manship entered into the picture, the live shows became bigger and better. Comedy, epitomized by Milton Berle in the early days, became an important part of the television diet. Sports were lured into television, and drama began to appear in increasing number if not always in increasing quality. Circuses and "kid shows" became more prominent; then games began to appear, and were rapidly accepted by the greatly increasing audience that was turning more and more to television as its principal source of entertainment and information. As the infant grew, however, the need for even greater quality and quantity of product became painfully evident; the creative efforts of the new broadcasters were taxed more and more each day. The cost of satisfying this growing appetite of the public for programming was subjugated to the great necessity for fulfilling this great need. So film product was bought, networks were expanded, local station time was multiplied—and all at substantial costs. The appetite had to be satisfied and the diet had to be good enough to attract constantly increasing audiences to provide the wherewithal to obtain more food for the growing appetite of the growing audience, and so on.

TELEVISION AS A BUSINESS

Television audiences did increase and the medium became attractive as a means of delivering commercial messages to large numbers of people in a manner unmatched in previous advertising history. Sales became the important factor. The need for attracting advertisers into the medium in larger and larger numbers became the important objective. The tremendous possibilities of television as a means of bringing advertising messages into the home, in addition to providing informative and entertaining programs, were delightfully evident and broadcasters leaped at the opportunity. This was the birth of television as a business—a business which could bring great good to the public, to advertisers and to the broadcasters.

For a while the rapid strides in the growth of television revenue were a pleasant sight to behold in the eyes of those who were responsible for operating television stations. The success of television was generally measured by the size of its sales increase.

In recent years, natural laws of economic behavior began to exert themselves and the medium finally matured into the *business* of television. As in every other business, the pressures of mounting costs, the great demand for product in ever increasing amounts and the problem of capacity in providing for commercially acceptable time periods made profitability a very important goal.

And so, the emphasis in television management shifted somewhat to a need for imaginative financial management of this "new business." The need for more creative programming, and for better and greater volume of public service programming, made it patently clear that expert financial management was required to provide a better balance between the medium of television and the business of television. The television station had to support its efforts in the production of public service programming as well as more and better entertainment programming, and yet provide a financial return commensurate with the risk involved to the shareholder. Every facet of television broadcasting became more expensive; the rise in the cost of doing business was even more rapid than the rise of the business itself. Cost awareness and the balanced control of costs became vital factors which required a great deal of attention and imaginative thinking if the medium was to grow to a healthy maturity. In many areas, television was being compared with other entertainment media; it was rapidly absorbing some of the high cost structure which had besieged those media—and persists in even greater degree today. Someone had to apply the measure of good business judgment to many of television's projects and practices. The controller, business manager or financial vice-president, was a natural choice to fill this need.

THE CONTROLLER AND MANAGEMENT

Traditionally, the controller in earlier years was a chief accountant and primarily limited himself to accounting responsibilities. Recording historical data was his principal function with little emphasis placed on the use of such data, to project what lay ahead. In a relatively short time, however, this function has expanded rapidly to include participation in the administration of the television station, involvement in labor negotiations and assistance in personnel development as well as, in many cases, training programs to help fill the need for more broadcasting management talent.

The controller's influence in the operation of the television station has been greatly enhanced and it is generally accepted that today his responsibilities include the following areas:

Recording the financial facts accurately—in accordance with generally accepted accounting principles and procedures established for his operation—the controller is responsible for maintaining an efficient and progressively informative accounts system. Rapid development of the medium and the need to more accurately reflect and establish the business position of the operation in any given period required revamping many of the old procedures. Established industry practices were woefully lacking in the treatment of various items. Amortization of film, depreciation of assets, and the accurate and effective joining together of income and respective cost elements within the same reporting period became more of a problem. The controller had to resolve these problems.

Reporting the historical financial facts of the station's activity, the controller analyzes the effects of these data and forecasts the financial impact of contemplated actions. He is responsible for realistically informing the station's management team of the financial result to be achieved in any programming, sales, promotion, publicity, engineering or other operation. To satisfy their own responsibility to the public, broadcasters must do many things which will not immediately enhance the profitability of a given television station. Nevertheless, it is essential that the financial yardstick be applied to all operations if intelligent financial planning is to accomplish an atmosphere of healthy growth.

Forecasting has become a necessity in television broadcasting because of the high cost of operation and because the profit margin is highly susceptible to unfavorable variations in an increasing sales pattern. There is a reasonably fixed level of operating costs which bears little or no relation to the amount of commercial business the station enjoys. Beyond this level of fixed costs, or "break-even volume," the television station can convert a substantial part of sales improvements to operating profit. Conversely, a drop-off in business is generally reflected in reduction in operating profit. It is essential, therefore, that for a healthy growth in profitability, the gross business improvement inherent in a young and dynamic industry contain within itself a satisfactory margin of profit. The measure of profitability must therefore be applied to new ventures in programming, promotion, facilities improvement and, in fact, to any other area designed to increase the gross revenue of a station. Because the size of an average television operation cannot justify a large analytical staff to measure the impact of contemplated projects or actions, the skill of the controller in applying his experience and knowledge to such problems can be an invaluable contribution to the general management.

The controller establishes and maintains internal control procedures necessary to protect the assets of the station, and to assure uniform compliance with administrative procedures and policies applicable to the total operation. Here again, the size of the accounting force available to the average controller does not allow comprehensive controls to be established. Ingenuity is required to work out an effective system which will reasonably safeguard the station's assets.

The controller supervises and coordinates the administrative activities of the organization except those directly concerned with the operating function of a department. Administration, which is so vitally a part of the general management of a station, cannot be allowed to subvert the principal responsibilities of the general manager. Because of the nature of his activity the controller is ideally suited to assume such administrative duties and, indeed, he should perform them.

In the average television operation, the controller must also maintain the facts needed for labor negotiations, and must develop a bargaining rapport with the general manager to form an effective negotiating team. The controller is the expert who interprets contracts and resolves differences within the station. He is the liaison with the upper echelons of the unions, both local and national. He must constantly be aware of the need for maintaining a harmonious relationship between management and the union which speaks for a substantial number of the operating people in a station. In recent years the improvement in wages and benefits of union employees has, in many cases, exceeded the rate of growth in a given operation; it requires great creative skill and effort to maintain a proper balance in these areas. The controller's background and training, in fact, make him ideally suited to undertake an important role in the labor relations inherent in television operation.

THE WORK OF THE CONTROLLER

In a typical television station, the controller's work will include such *specific* duties as those listed below.

Accounting: Install and supervise the maintenance of all accounting records on an up-to-date basis. Audit and review all accounts for conformity with generally accepted accounting and financial principles, and with procedures established for the station. Select and train subordinates. Plan and schedule the work load of the accounting staff so as to permit continuity of results even under adverse conditions. Supervise all payroll activities and the maintenance of such records as are normally required. Establish the credit position with proper payment procedures designed to maintain the station's financial reputation while, at the same time, obtaining maximum use of funds.

Controls and Budgets: Establish internal control procedures which are necessary to the safeguarding of corporate assets, and continuously evaluate them. Establish a coordinated capital expenditures program and supervise its operation in such a way as to provide optimum use of assets while also allowing maximum equipment capability for the station. Assist in the preparation of individual departmental budgets, and prepare a consolidated budget for the over-all operation as a means of measuring performance in each fiscal period.

Industrial Relations: Develop statistical data, including comparative market figures, for use in union negotiations. Analyze offers and demands to determine the financial impact of each, and participate in union negotiations. Supervise the final preparation of labor union contracts, and keep all associates informed of the provisions of such union agreements. Handle union grievances not immediately solvable by department heads. Supervise arbitration when necessary.

Personnel: Establish salary scales as a guide for station operation. Supervise the hiring and firing of clerical people, in conjunction with the appropriate department heads. Administer employee benefit plans, and handle all claims and problems relating thereto.

Credit Control: Establish and maintain a policy of credit extension compatible with maximum sales effort and reasonable, though not always minimal risks. Maintain a direct relationship with the station's customers that is conducive to satisfactory credit and collection procedures. Establish rapport with other credit people as a source of general credit information and control. Participate in insolvency or bankruptcy proceedings where necessary.

Office Management: Establish and supervise the operation of necessary communication systems including telephone, teletype, messenger service, etc. Procure all administrative and clerical supplies, furniture and equipment, supervise custodial maintenance of the entire physical plant. Negotiate reciprocal arrangements for needed merchandise or services.

Administrative Management: Analyze ratings and prepare data suitable for study and interpretation by the interested department heads. (Unless there is a Research Department—Ed.) Establish a plan for employee vacations providing minimum disruption of station operation.

Financial Management: Establish a system of cost control, in collaboration with the general manager, and supervise the operation of such system. In conjunction with the Sales Department, establish rate cards conducive to maximum business and profit. Prepare reports as required (monthly, quarterly, annual) analyzing the financial status of the organization, and measuring performance against the financial objectives. Keep current on all tax requirements in connection with the station's operation, and prepare all necessary tax returns. Determine and maintain needed insurance protection for all physical assets. As treasurer of the station, maintain control of all funds and invest excess funds so as to obtain maximum return.

THE ACCOUNTING DEPARTMENT

The organizational structure of a television station may vary from market to market depending on the size of the station, its profitability, or whether it is an independent or part of multi-station ownership, a group operation, or a network. The number of people in the Accounting Department may vary from as few as three to as many as 15 or 20. In a station operating with a network affiliation in a medium size market, seven people are generally required if the controller is to perform all the financial functions necessary to its successful operation. At such a station, the department may consist of a controller, an assistant, accounting supervisor, payroll supervisor, a secretary and two clerks. Under such an organization, the controller will assume over-all responsibility for the functions indicated in the preceding pages of this chapter. The assistant controller is responsible for the entire accounting operation of the department with direct supervision of the handling of all accounting and financial data, the recording of these data and the preparation of financial statements for use by various echelons of management.

The accounting supervisor, or the billing supervisor as he may be called in some operations, is essentially responsible for the billing to advertisers and agencies. In this area he is assisted by a billing clerk who checks the station logs and posts the daily business transactions to such records as are necessary to accumulate the data for billing at the end of a given month. Orders, time sales and facilities charges must be set up in such a manner that posting of the daily transactions can be handled expeditiously. The billing supervisor also is responsible for preparing a listing of unbilled orders, which serves as a valuable tool for comparing the volume of business in the house at a given time with the same period of the prior year. The sales manager and the general manager are constantly striving to improve the sales position of the station, and it is important to know at frequent intervals whether these efforts are meeting with success. A projection of unbilled orders can be an important help in evaluating sales activity.

Discrepencies occasionally develop between the order as it was placed and as it was delivered. The accounting supervisor is responsible for providing complete information to the advertising agency to encourage the agency to make payment despite unavoidable variations from the contract. This area is becoming increasingly important since agencies have generally adopted the philosophy of "putting aside" invoices reflecting performance which does not meticulously and in total agree with the order as it was placed. Quite frequently discrepancies which have been previously cleared with a time buyer at the agency have not been documented with the department charged with the responsibility of clearing the bills for payment. In many cases these situations develop because of the complexity of the agency operation, and often because of the lack of sufficient communication between the broadcaster and the agency. Here the accounting supervisor can be of definite aid in furnishing invoices that have adequate explanation and documentation, and so enable the agency to reconcile any differences and make immediate payment.

The payroll supervisor is responsible for the payment of salaries and wages to all employees of the station. He also prepares such other records as are required on payments made to employees as compensation or benefits. The preparation of social security reports, and such reports as may be required by insurance companies in connection with employee benefits, are also his responsibility. The payroll supervisor must be thoroughly familiar with all federal, state and local laws pertaining to wages and hours of employment. He must maintain all required records and must work with wage and hour inspectors during their periodic examinations.

Two other clerks are required to handle the variety of accounting activities. A typical distribution of responsibility might have one clerk handling such items as: petty cash, general ledger posting, accounts-payable checks and posting, distribution of talent charges, cash reports and statements, and allied reports pertaining to these functions. A second clerk may handle accounts receivable, posting and settlement, and purchase orders. He may also match invoices and purchase orders and authenticate bills for payment, as well as check out bills and code bills for proper accounting treatment. In addition, this clerk may handle the entries necessary to establish film amortization, the accrual entries, and the entries for prepaid items; further, he may prepare such documents and reports as accounts receivable aging analysis, open purchase orders, etc.

The seventh member of the department is a secretary who

may handle all the industrial relations functions of the Accounting Department. These include insurance claims, hospitalization claims, and similar matters pertaining to employee-benefit programs established by the station. These responsibilities are in addition to the normal secretarial duties required by the controller and other members of the department.

In a larger operation, it may be necessary to provide additional people to handle certain of the duties that are combined in the above job descriptions. In a smaller station, where the size and number of transactions may be somewhat reduced, it is possible to combine even further the job responsibilities of certain employees.

PROGRAMMING AND THE CONTROLLER

While it is true that every department head must be aware of the over-all profitability of a station, it is not necessarily inherent in the function of operating departments to provide for increased profitability in the general operation. In programming and production particularly, the need for creative work must not be subjugated entirely to the profit motive. The program manager must be responsible for the operation of his department so as to contribute to the over-all effectiveness of the station; but essentially, his department is concerned with creating product and exhibiting product in a manner designed to provide maximum audience for each segment of the broadcast day. In view of this, the controller should work closely with the members of the Program Department in evaluating and guiding their efforts to the end that their best creative work is produced at a level of cost which will allow the desired margin of profitability from a given project. There are many ways to produce a program and each different way entails a different element of cost. For example, a given show may require original artwork as a prop for the right background and atmosphere. On the other hand, it is entirely possible that in similar shows a reproduction will give the same effect and atmosphere at a substantially reduced cost. In the area of talent, the program manager is generally desirous of obtaining the best available for a given role. Here too, however, it is necessary that reasonable limitations be placed upon the amount of money available for such talent. The same comparison applies to almost the entire operation, and a good controller will stimulate the members of the Programming Department to arrive at the desired level of creative achievement at the lowest possible cost. The controller should establish rapport with the program manager and production manager and should be a welcomed member at the final session to consider a program project. His advice and counsel should be sought and, in turn, his contribution should be positive and valuable. The final level of creative product must be compatible with the desired goal and the economic possibility of its achievement.

SALES AND THE CONTROLLER

It is the controller's responsibility to work closely with the sales manager, too, to make certain that the time rates established provide sufficient margin of profitability and that sales policies in connection with rates are effectively followed. It is the controller, in the final analysis, who must make certain that an improvement in sales volume will be a *profitable* improvement. Moreover, in conjunction with the Engineering Department and Program Department, the controller should also establish satisfactory rates, where required, for the use of facilities and for such other program costs as are reasonably chargeable to the advertiser. Such rates must be competitive and, at the same time, profitable.

In recent years, a number of television stations have adopted the short-sighted policy of "cutting rates." This is often done in an attempt to get business which cannot otherwise be obtained because of an insufficiency of audience or station stature. Where these practices are followed, the importance of the controller's over-all supervision is even more vital because unprofitable sales can very easily be the result. The controller should be an influential voice in maintaining the integrity of a rate position that is equitable in providing advertising efficiency to the client at a figure that will allow a reasonable profit to the station.

PROMOTION AND THE CONTROLLER

A product once well planned and produced must be promoted to be effectively sold. But there are various ways in which the product and the station can be brought to the attention of the public, the agencies and advertisers. It is not difficult to *buy* promotion and publicity; indeed, in many cases, such costs may necessarily be substantial. The experience and guidance of the controller, however, should be a strong force in persuading the Promotion and Publicity Department to obtain these important elements of a station operation at a low cost or, in some instances, at no cost. As with the other functions inherent in television broadcasting, a promotion or publicity campaign must be scrutinized from the viewpoint of measuring the goal to be achieved against the cost of reaching that goal.

ENGINEERING AND THE CONTROLLER

The rapid advances in technology in the television industry make it very difficult to maintain a proper balance between facility improvement and the contribution to profit that results. Obsolescence is a factor that must be considered, yet too little use of a facility can be as injurious as too much use of the same equipment asset. Broadcasting is as susceptible to gadgetry in engineering as are other industries. Obviously, the station must be equipped in a manner which will allow it to be competitive in its market place. The measure of this competition, however, must be judged by the result that is reflected on the television screen in the viewer's home and it does not require a one-for-one match with every item of equipment existing in the competitive station. Full use of engineering facilities must be obtained while, at the same time, there must be implemented a program of reasonable modernization sufficient to keep abreast of important equipment changes. Here again, the measure of profitability must be applied.

PROBLEMS OF THE CONTROLLER

Because the controller's responsibilities have been among the last major functions in a television station to receive emphasis, there are numerous problems inherent in the management of his department. Primarily, the controller must overcome a natural tendency on the part of operating personnel to look upon members of his staff and of the Accounting Department as "green eyeshade men." To combat this, he must endeavor to foster more general understanding of and respect for the valuable contribution to the orderly (and profitable) operation of the television station that the controller's work can make.

Cost reduction is a means of fighting the "squeeze" resulting from the continuing trend of rising costs, and this is another problem for the controller. But there is a certain stigma attached to the term and it is often resisted, particularly in a television station—perhaps because it runs counter to the nature of the television function. In view of this, therefore, the controller must aim to establish an atmosphere of "cost awareness." Whereas cost reduction seems to carry with it the idea that reductions are to be made regardless of their impact on the over-all operation, the concept of *cost awareness* is entirely different as it connotes merely that at some stage of the development of a project, or a campaign, or in the consideration of new facilities equipment, the measure of profitability must be applied.

Selling the concept of cost awareness, however, is not a simple task. To be effective, the controller must have achieved sufficient stature through his own ability and performance to impress the operating heads with his understanding of the detailed operations of the station and appreciation of their specific problems. Such familiarity with operational practice is a prerequisite to intelligent discussion with each functional department, and to the guidance or direction that can lead to greater profitability. Essentially, then, the controller must constantly sell the idea of profitability to personnel who may be more concerned with, or immersed in, creative or technical accomplishments.

SUMMARY

It is evident that a controller's range of responsibilities may be extensive. In the average television station, he performs many functions that would be delegated to others in larger and more substantial businesses. He may be at once a treasurer, industrial relations manager, systems and procedures manager, credit manager, budget director, personnel manager, office manager, payroll supervisor, and even research director. The controller must, therefore, be experienced in all these areas; he must posses sufficient background and judgment for sound decisions in each of his numerous functions.

In short, the controller is the financial representative of the management team of a television station; he is the man primarily responsible for translating the contributions of the operating departments into a profitable business. As the financial specialist of the staff, he must coax the maximum profitability compatible with realization of the operation's creative efforts. His is the function of helping to blend product and professional achievement into a profitable framework.

PART THREE

PROGRAMMING, PRODUCTION,
PUBLICITY

CHAPTER 7

Programming for the Commercial Station

BY EDWARD A. WARREN

Now Program Director for the American Broadcasting Company's owned-and-operated television stations, Mr. Warren was formerly Program Director of WNBC-TV in New York and, before that, WGN-TV in Chicago. A native of Philadelphia, he majored in drama at Catholic University in Washington, D. C., and later became a professor of drama and communication arts at St. Mary's College, Notre Dame.

THE theater tends to appeal to specialized audiences while the circus, by contrast, seeks a broader base. Motion pictures and radio are more or less in between, appealing to the general public but doing so through varied programming. Television tends to reach out in a combination of these patterns. And whether one is programming an independent station, a network-affiliated station, or a network-owned station, the basic principles will remain the same, varying only in degree or in style.

Consciously or unconsciously one faces the problem: "How do I 'sell tickets' to the right people at the right time, 18 hours a day, seven days a week, 52 weeks a year?" In other words, how does the program director get the available American public to watch his television station to the greatest possible extent? Moreover, the problem, certainly overwhelming enough inherently, must be faced while at the same time attending to such matters as costs, profits, parent-company relationships, a limited staff, perhaps the ups and downs of network service, and those promises the station made to the FCC.

PRINCIPLES OF PROGRAMMING

1. Know Your Audience: There is no point in programming in the abstract. Programming must be responsive to the interests of one's community. A program manager must know his total audience, know its components, and know when they are available to view. This requires considerable sophistication. One has to be aware of regional interests within the community. On the other hand, it must be remembered that the American taste does not change much from Seattle to Jacksonville. One must be responsive to the community's leaders, intellectuals, and special interest groups; and at the same time be aware that, as important as these interests are, they do not represent the total audience.

The program manager must use research to know his audience. He must know what happens in the community's homes throughout the day, what time the men leave, at what time the women are most busy, when they are available for viewing, when various age groups of children are available, what viewing changes take place on Saturday, on Sunday, in prime evening time, and late at night. There is much in programming that appeals to the broad base of the American public but, on the other hand, there are many regional differences. One case in point is the fact that, on the west coast, late-night viewing is virtually non-existent, whereas in the mid-west and east stations can program successfully into the early morning hours. Such a major difference in viewing patterns will greatly influence program planning, purchasing and production, and the subsequent economics of the whole television station.

2. Know Your Product: The program director should be interested in and have a working knowledge of the entire history of show business. He should have a good liberal arts education, with an awareness of basic principles of dramatic, literary, and aesthetic criticism. In his day-to-day work he should be thoroughly familiar with all available programming from syndicated television shows, to special feature material, to motion pictures. He should also be acquainted with all local programming possibilities, from cultural performances to sports events. Programming requires life-long education, learning, and self-informing.

3. Know Your Competition: Programming is not only designed to appeal to potential viewers intrinsically. It must also be more appealing than what one's competition offers, and the alert program manager should be watchful of the activities of his competitors. He should know what programs and films they buy, what talent they hire, even what sales they make inasmuch as a time sale might be a catalyst for a program acquisition for a certain client. Then, being knowledgeable about the activities of his competitors, the program manager must move to counteract those efforts with his own program selections.

4. *Know Your Budgets:* The program manager should be familiar with all of the profit-and-loss problems of all parts of the day. Each segment of the programming day should be isolated in terms of budget requirements so that the program manager can know the minimum and maximum limits of the total budget that can be applied toward those time periods. Furthermore, projections should be made with the sales manager or business manager to determine the maximum income possible if, for example, the respective programs were to be 50% sold, or 75% sold, and so on. The program manager must be realistic in his activities, not feigning ultra-conservatism that results in shoddy production, and at the same time not being euphoric in his ambitions to the extent that his programming cannot be sustained by sales. He must understand his financial restrictions and possibilities and do the best job within those realities.

5. *Know Your Staff:* A program manager should have a staff he respects and trusts, and who will effectively assume delegated responsibility. The staff should keep on-the-air operation clean and professional, without blunders. They should generate ideas and suggestions. These are the men who are responsible for what people literally see the station doing. If this performance is not first rate, there should be no hesitancy about changing personnel.

6. *Know Your Community:* It takes time and much contact work to be involved with one's community. Therefore, it may be advantageous to have an inside man and an outside man. Mr. Inside can keep the station on the air. Mr. Outside can represent the station at the community luncheons and cocktail parties, learning the attitudes of the community leaders and reporting them back to the station management. A television station is a conspicuous

and leading member of its society and it is important that it be intimately involved in the thinking, planning, and activities of that community.

7. *Know Your Management:* The program manager can function best when he intelligently understands how he relates to the total operation of the television station. He should know his sales manager and that man's problems; if they can establish a close working relationship it is possible that each may realize his respective goals more successfully than either had anticipated. The program manager must also understand the general manager, his over-all responsibilities, and his need for honest and objective program advice. A good program manager will not be a yes-man, but he will also be mindful that he is not the general manager and that the total responsibility does rest elsewhere.

8. *Know Yourself:* The entire station's livelihood depends on sales which, in turn, depends on programming. Almost everyone at the station will have suggestions for the program manager who should, of course, be several steps ahead of everyone in his special area. On the other hand, he must not let pride of authorship or friendship stand in the way of objectivity. If there is programming that is getting low ratings, critical blame, or is causing concern among associates, the program manager should check the show and re-check his research. Perhaps production can be improved. Maybe the problem is in casting. Maybe the time period is wrong. Maybe the program is not compatible with the preceding program and therefore does not have sufficient opportunity to get an audience. A program manager should be honest enough with himself to reconsider prior decisions and judgments.

THE FUNCTIONS OF PROGRAMMING

No two programming jobs are the same. Each station management group has its own particular goals and methods that it brings to broadcasting, and therefore the programming function will reflect these differences. In some cases, management will be extremely public-service-minded. Others will be largely creative. Still others will have little interest in broadcasting beyond the commercial. Naturally these attitudes will influence the activities and potentialities of the program manager.

The scope and responsibility of the program manager's job is much greater at an independent station, of course, where there can be more than 125 hours a week of programming needed. At a station owned by or affiliated with a network, programming often is just a pushbutton away; but even here there are many hours of product needed, as well as the acumen necessary to integrate a network service into the ambience of a local community.

Nevertheless, the similarities are greater than the differences. For example, any program manager encounters a great amount of administrative detail that frequently can be handled by a competent secretary acting in the role of an administrative assistant. The few extra dollars necessary for a secretary of this caliber can free the program man for more important creative and management functions. There is also a need for a competent person to handle the detail regarding film programming. Film programs must be screened for content, must be timed, must be prepared for on-the-air use. All this requires copiously detailed information, especially at an independent station where film is used in such great quantity.

The actual buying of the film may be done by the general manager, the program manager, or the film director. The decision for this policy is usually that of the general manager and reflects his own interest in the selection, programming, and bargaining for film programs. It is this writer's recommendation, however, that film buying be handled by a qualified film director who thoroughly understands the programming, production, and financial aspects of that function.

With regard to live programming, there should be an executive producer responsible for the entire operation. He should be concerned not only with day-to-day activity but with program development as well. There should also be a public affairs director to handle programming of a community nature. Of course, many of these functions are in gray areas and will vary from station to station, so that some executive producers may take care of public affairs programming, and some member of management may take care of film buying. The important thing is to recognize the specific responsibilities that must be attended to, and to assign to them persons who are competent in those respective areas.

In any case, these are the functions. The broad activity is programming that reflects the needs of the community and the station, and the interests of the management. An independent station has a difficult job because it does not have the strength of the often popular and well produced network fare. On the other hand, having no commitment to a network, the independent station can move more freely in acquiring and scheduling syndicated film programs, feature films, sports events of particular local interest, and other special events. Thus, an independent station may in various times of the day out-rate its network-affiliated competitors.

A network affiliate, though not having as much flexibility, can also express its personality in its non-network hours, as well as in its occasional pre-emptions of network fare for special programs of its own. The network-owned stations have a greater commitment to carry their company's programming, but even they have the opportunity for original productions. Within these respective frameworks, the program managers pursue their activities with a common concern and a primary responsibility for what goes on the air and where the programs are scheduled.

THE BROADCAST DAY

There is a theory in programming that a station can hold its audience from sign-on to sign-off. This is a carry-over from radio days, and assumes that the audience the station gets in the morning stays with it throughout the entire broadcast day. It further assumes that if one's station is the last one viewed at night, it is likely to be viewed the first thing in the morning because the dial has not changed. Unfortunately, while there is an element of truth (and something of advantage) in this, the premise was more relevant to radio. Television is a more selective medium and there is a tendency for the viewer, after a half hour, or an hour, or some such span of time, to check to see what is available on some other station. It is the job of the Program Department to minimize this tendency to tune-out, by anticipating the programming interests of the public as those interests change throughout the day.

For example, it is generally accepted that the television set is used as an electronic baby-sitter during the early morning hours. After the school children have left for the day, the pre-schoolers are available to watch a children's program. Therefore, if a station has a nursery school program, or cartoons, or some such fare it will generally be a strong rating contender in this time period. And this also serves to get the set tuned on to that station, giving it an advantage for later programming. Now, if the children's programming is followed up with situation comedies that are filled with action, the station will tend to keep much of this same audience and begin to add adults. However, if the children's programming is followed by a woman's talk-show on fashions, the station will lose the children and have to depend on a new audience arriving, a "tune-in" audience. This is always a difficult matter, and even more so at the mid-morning time of day when the network game shows are beginning. The basic idea remains, however, to program to satisfy those persons available who are inclined to view television. This must be further refined to be competitive vis à vis the other stations in the market. The tactics can become still more sophisticated as one programs not only to counteract competition but even draw off from the competitor's preceding program. Even this effort is not enough, however, for one must also seek to program to reach eventually the greatest possible adult audience, for it is this group of viewers that is the most saleable to the advertisers.

The next major period of local program time occurs in the noon area. Again, the children provide the possibility for large audiences with a lunchtime cartoon or entertainment program hosted by a Bozo the Clown or an Uncle Bill or Whom Have You. On the other hand, if the station can be successful with an appealing news program at noon, it will be able to garner considerably more advertiser revenue. Another alternative is the situation comedy which would appeal to both adults and children. *Our Miss Brooks, Margie, Bachelor Father,* and programs of that nature have done well in this time period. By one o'clock it is time for programming that provides emotional adventure for the adult female audience that is available, and so begin the soap operas and the dramatic programs.

The next important time period is from four or five o'clock until seven-thirty, depending upon the station's allocation of local time. This can be programmed strictly for adults with feature films or hour-long dramatic programs, followed by news. Not only is such adult programming highly saleable, but it is also important to provide a strong lead-in for that time of the day when television viewership is at its peak, the prime-time evening hours between seven-thirty and eleven o'clock. Some stations, of course, build for

that lead-in with children's programming. These commercial availabilities are particularly saleable during the fourth quarter of the
year because of the toy business, and to some extent there is significant saleability throughout the rest of the year. But the potential
of children's programming does not equal that of adult fare. On
the other hand, if one's competitor is strongly entrenched in that
time period with adult programming, attractive children's programs may be the best move available.

The final period of local programming generally follows network service. At ten or eleven o'clock, most stations begin their
late night service with news, both for its service value and for its
saleability. The success of this program is dependent on the quality
of the writing and the personality of the on-the-air newsman. There
must be an appealing combination in the selection of stories and
the emphasis, pace, and rhythm of their presentation.

Many stations also program a brief weather spot and here,
especially, the personality of the performer is paramount. The
production is usually low-budget and the gimmicks are few, so the
whole appeal rests on the way that weatherman or weather gal says
that it is 78 degrees outside. People claim that they do not like to
hear about highs and lows, and isobars, and cold fronts and warm
fronts. All they want to know is if it is going to rain tomorrow or
if it is going to be cold tonight so that they can dress appropriately
and decide whether they should put an extra blanket on the children. It should be pointed out, however, that one of the main reasons for the five-minute weather show is for its saleability. Therefore, there is a need for that esoteric meteorology that is included
in the weathercast, for it provides something to say around the commercials.

Sports news frequently follows the weather, providing another
highly saleable program, as well as the occasion for another spot
announcement between programs. During the baseball and football
seasons, sports receive continuing attention. When it is off-season,
the sports personality is put to his hardest test in keeping the audience interested.

The length of the news-weather-sports combination should be
determined by the time necessary to get into the station's major
late-night program, which will generally be a feature film or else a
talk show such as *Tonight*. A station should try to capture the late

night audience by starting its major program a few minutes before the competition's, thus giving that station the first opportunity to seize the audience. Furthermore, the need to try to take the audience away from a long program on the competition, in which it has already become involved, is obviated. At the very least, begin the late night program even with your competition, but never after his programming has begun.

FEATURE FILM SCHEDULING

The scheduling and handling of late night feature films is a serious activity. Everyone feels he is a movie expert, although few persons are. While one might understand principles of cinema, their effectiveness on television can only be predicted from experience. For example, a top grosser at the box office might not be successful when played on television five years later. Musical comedies, no matter how successful at the theater, are practically always rating failures on television. Many stations schedule films by reading a synopsis of the plot and recognizing a few names in the cast. This is not sufficient. All features should be screened before they are scheduled, regardless of what some early review says and regardless of their box office records.

When features are shown at night, they should reveal the actual story as quickly as possible. They should begin with the first frame of interest so as to get the viewer's attention before he tunes out—the station can superimpose the title of the film and the names of its stars. The important thing is to lead with action. Other titles and credits can be run at the end. Commercial interruptions should be limited to no more than one every 15 minutes. Furthermore, a feature film should not be re-run for at least a year. Many stations will re-run films after only six months, and often this is necessary because of the limitation of product. The longer period is more desirable, however.

Another sale may be possible with a late-late news wrapup that can be done inexpensively by a booth announcer speaking over slides. The lateness of programming will depend on the potentiality of finding late-night viewers which, as was observed, is greater in the mid-west and east than in the far west.

WEEKEND PROGRAMMING

Saturday morning is the meeting place of virtually every children's personality and cartoon character extant, plus a few that had appeared to have been left far in the past. The afternoon may bring a local sporting event, such as high school football, or there may be a feature film. And then, back to the network.

On Sunday morning there are usually religious programs, followed by an early afternoon foray into educational and informational programs. These serve to meet FCC requirements, elicit publicity, and perform well-intended services. Sunday afternoon may bring on a feature film or network sports.

The late-night programming on the weekend is similar to the rest of the week.

COUNTER-PROGRAMMING

While the programming patterns that have been examined are rather prevalent, there are always different concepts that can be tried. But whether different or commonplace, programming often benefits by being scheduled in time periods when the competition has a different type of show. This "counter-programming" can give a station an excellent opportunity to reach a totally different audience instead of dividing up the limited audience already viewing.

The research man at the local station should make a study of audience flow so that the program manager can know where the audience is at any given time, where it came from, where it goes, and when it does leave. (See Chapter 12 in this connection—Ed.) If such a study shows that at a certain hour a station's share of audience suddenly drops, it is obvious that some changes are needed. In a sense, programming is like a bridge game. A good program manager will know how to play his strong programming well, and how to slough losing programs.

SUMMARY

Not every programming decision is made by a program director. Frequently, they are made by sales managers or general managers; and sometimes they are made by less obvious sources, such as critics or wives. Some sales managers do have a background in programming, but most general managers have come up from sales; only a very few wives have had programming experience.

This writer once ordered the rescheduling of some dramatic plays, so as to avoid an unfortunate conflict with a religious holiday. In the rescheduling, someone marked down *Medea* for a Sunday evening that turned out to be Mother's Day—a good example of bad programming! Actually, programming is many things: a knowledge of people, viewing habits, and research. It is an understanding of one's management, and an attentiveness to the competition. It is the courage of one's convictions and the respect for those of one's colleagues. It is, in the final analysis, judgment. It is subjective. And it can be wrong. The idea is to be right most of the time.

CHAPTER 8

Programming for the Educational Television Station

BY VERNON F. COOK

WYES-TV, New Orleans, Louisiana

Program Manager of New Orleans community educational television station, WYES-TV, since its beginning in 1957, Mr. Cook spent many years as a performer before trading his place before the cameras for a creative role behind the scenes. While a student at Syracuse University, he was associated with the NBC affiliate in that city, and in 1947 joined the staff of the General Electric Company's pioneer television station in Schenectady, New York. Mr. Cook has said that his experience as a performer and later as a supervisor in advertising agency television has served him well in his programming work in ETV.

P ROGRAM pathways of the educational television station are particularly fraught with pitfalls. And the program manager, beset with advice, suggestions and outright demands, must to a great extent rely on intuition to avoid the pratfalls. The general manager of the station has the ultimate responsibility and on occasion his intuition, too, is involved. In particularly knotty cases he may also consult with his Board of Directors. However, the primary responsibility for what goes on the air remains with the program director.

Educational television in the United States is intended for in-school instruction at all levels, and for extensive community service. This can, indeed should, encompass the cultural, informational, recreational, political, social and moral areas to the extent that these are part of the fiber of the community. Stations operated by school boards or universities are sometimes inclined to accent formal instruction in their schedules to help cope with the teacher shortage, classroom shortage or both. Esoteric subjects or a course in typing at 8 P.M. are not uncommon. This may seem to be a questionable use of such valuable TV time, but these licensees can justifiably point to their tax or educational foundation support and prove without question that they are following sound educational dictates. But, this is not to say that these same schedules will not generally reflect an alertness to community problems and subjects of general interest. Every educational station is a library, and the arrangement of the program material in the schedule is a matter of both choice and necessity. Generally the most popular books, or programs, should be convenient for easy access.

The program manager of a school board or university-owned station may have less opportunity to exercise his initiative than his counterpart on a community station. The reasons are understandable and justifiable. An institution which surrenders program prerogatives is liable to find itself with a TV image which does not reflect its traditions or general policy. Both terms are difficult to define but not too difficult to flout. Hence, the cautions.

PROGRAMMING FOR THE COMMUNITY STATION

The community station, on the other hand, enjoys greater freedom of choice because of the greater availability of time. And so it is the role of the program manager of the community station that is of most interest. Inevitably, he is restricted from programming with a lavish hand, as compared to commercial broadcasters, due to a lack of sufficient funds. However, there are instances of underwriters (businesses, foundations, private donors) providing funds for dressed-up productions on community stations. Further, there are the programs syndicated to all of the ETV stations throughout the country through the facilities of National Educational Television in New York, the acceptability of which is virtually a foregone conclusion. Programming the remaining time periods for the community at large with his limited funds, is essentially the major role of the program manager of the community ETV station. Program resource material and personnel are dictated largely by the size and sophistication of the community in question, but there are obvious resources which are common to all.

GOVERNMENT AS PROGRAM SOURCES

One of these sources is government, the great number of elected and appointed officials from the city, the county and the state. Programs concerning government should be approached from a scrupulously objective viewpoint and with a certain built-in wariness. The impulse of people in political life is to justify their positions to the electorate at every reasonable opportunity. The station, therefore, must be diligent in maintaining its independence.

For example, let us suppose a civic center is the pet project of a certain administration and time is requested to describe it in detail to the community. It is not likely that the administration in question will invite those whom they know to be critical of the idea to participate in the program. It is, therefore, up to the program manager to take the program request under advisement and to find out for himself if there is opposition, how responsible it is, and how, let us say, the mayor will react to the suggestion that his foe in the last election be permitted to share the television platform with him. If the mayor has a strong case, he may welcome the opportunity. On the other hand, he may feel that, by virtue of his election, he has a right to speak without having to cope with a dissident voice. It is almost always best to have opposing factions at the same time in order to avoid being whipsawed between one group and the other.

LOCAL ISSUES AS PROGRAM SOURCES

Another source of programming exists in local issues in which the community is interested. Information and participants in prospective television shows are readily available from the groups or organizations that may be particularly concerned, such as: the League of Women Voters; the American Association of University Women; the American Association of University Professors; the Chamber of Commerce; the American Institute of Architects; the American Medical Association; and the American Dental Association, to mention just a few. Fluoridation, academic freedom, the liberal-conservative debate, reapportionment and redistricting, are but a sampling of the pro and con subjects which can be given a

certain stamp of approval as far as program concept and participants are concerned when they are presented in cooperation with
one or several such organizations.

OTHER PROGRAM SOURCES

The art, music, literary and theater groups are also valuable program sources. They are generally conscientious and appreciative,
and the time spent in indoctrinating them in the rudiments of preparing a program for television is usually time well spent. Similarly, there is a wealth of material available from the educational
institutions, museums, and libraries.

Programming with religious groups should be approached, if
at all, through the qualified organizations which represent the various denominations, Protestant, Catholic and Jewish. These organizations, despite their differences in dogma or approach to the spir-
itual, seem to bear a genuine good will toward one another and this
is reflected in the positive way in which they treat their subject.

The individual zealot, on the other hand, may have his own
reasons for not professing within any of the above groups, and no
one questions his freedom not to align himself. But it is a completely
defensible attitude to question his claim to television time to express
his personal convictions. Credentials and qualifications must be the
guide to the programmer who is confronted with the request for
"time to air my views."

The programming of athletic competitions is occasionally crit-
icized by individuals; and when it is, it is marked by vehemence.
It is handy at such times to refer to the Groves of Academe or *mens
sana in corpore sano*. If this doesn't pacify the complainant, one
might refer to the President's Council on Physical Fitness and the
station's active encouragement of such principles.

LIVING COMMUNICATION

Perhaps one of educational television's best opportunities is in
a modernization of the classic New England town meeting. Here
was provided a forum for the interchange of ideas that had dramatic impact by virtue of the meeting's simplicity, acknowledged
freedoms and small stage concept. With the advent of the me-
tropolis, this opportunity for discourse and the opportunity to
hear a broad diversity of opinion suffered. The marvel of tele-

vision's electronic communication has re-established the opportunity for that exchange in an intimacy even more compelling than in the original form. The one-to-one relationship in this TV miracle is awesome in its power.

Perhaps the most difficult area of programming for educational television is in the field of emotionally charged issues. Here the community station, as in the area of politics, is in a position to perform the valuable town forum function. Such programming must be approached with deep understanding and with recognition of responsibility to the community and to the total situation. The criteria should be timeliness and usefulness, a balance of representative opinion across the spectrum, and a deliberate hope or intention that ventilation of the subject may reduce some of the heat and add some light.

The program manager of a community educational television station must be responsive to the needs and aspirations of his station's viewers, to serve those viewers imaginatively and courageously in the areas of information, education, culture and civic affairs. His audience may not be as large as he would wish, and certainly his budget will not be as big as he would like. But one thing he need never worry about being in short supply will be the needs of the community that he serves.

CHAPTER 9

Production Management

BY COLBY LEWIS

Michigan State University

Professor of Television and Radio and Coordinator of Closed Circuit Television at Michigan State University, Mr. Lewis is involved in television production as a teacher, administrator and producer. He was formerly Production Manager of WTTW, Chicago's educational television station, and Assistant Program Manager of WTMJ-TV, the *Milwaukee Journal* station in Milwaukee, Wisconsin.

MANAGING the production of local programs is something with which a production manager may have little or much to do. If a station does not originate much local programming, there may be no need for him at all, since the program manager can find time both to schedule the programs and supervise their production. When the schedule is somewhat more active, the production manager may exist, but only to assist the program manager as supervisor of studios, staging, and lighting. In some of the most active stations, he may rank on a level with the program manager and manage the whole process of translating a program from paper or from someone's mind into the actual sights and sounds which are fed to the cameras and microphones.

In managing this process, he may coordinate the work of a number of job categories which do not report to him. Staging, lighting, scene design, and graphics will commonly fall within his jurisdiction. Film production, however, may come under programming, since a film director's primary responsibility is to handle program film; and sometimes, if the film produced is mainly news film, its production will be in charge of the news director. Television cameramen, particularly in unionized stations, are likely to be engineers, but in some stations where they are chosen primarily for their sense of timing and pictorial composition, they are production people. Some stations employ producers to conceive and plan the content of programs (a programming matter) and to exercise general supervision over their execution (which is surely a production matter). Who is their immediate superior? Sometimes the production manager—sometimes not.

It is fruitless to continue these qualifications. Happily, there is a way to avoid them. Wherever activities are placed in the station's pattern of organization, there is still the need to coordinate their contributions to the production process. This job must be done by one or more persons, whatever their title. And so this chapter will speak less about the production manager than about the job of production management.

THE GENERAL NATURE OF PRODUCTION MANAGEMENT

Roughly speaking, production begins at whatever stage a program may be when the program manager has scheduled it—perhaps as an outline, perhaps as an already rehearsed performance which an outside producer has brought into the station to be put on camera. It terminates when light and sound waves from the performance become electrical signals within the province of the chief engineer.

Throughout this course the production of each single program is guided by its producer and director or, more commonly, by a person who combines these offices under the title of producer-director. The producer-director selects the performers and their material, plans and orders various other program ingredients, devises the sound and camera treatment, and, during the broadcast or video recording, coordinates all the activity of performers and technicians.

But someone must supervise the producer-directors and maintain the conditions they need for their work. They could accomplish little without an efficient supply of supporting resources: studios, sets, lights, music, graphics, film inserts, cameras, microphones, and various kinds of operating personnel; and all of these resources must be assembled at the proper state of readiness and at the proper time, not only for one program but for many.

The station can be thought of as a kind of manufacturing plant, in which several products may be on the assembly line at the same time. This plant must have the proper human and physical resources to turn out its products. It must operate according to certain standards and orderly procedures. Its resources must be scheduled and apportioned between the various jobs on the line. The quality of these jobs must be controlled. Their costs must be accounted for and kept within tolerances that may allow the station, if educational, to remain solvent, and if commercial, to realize a profit. These are the concerns of production management. They will now be described in more detail.

ESTABLISHING THE PRODUCTION REQUIREMENTS

Whenever a new program is scheduled for production, all concerned should understand its aims and what, in general, they will contribute to it.

This knowledge can be provided either by interpersonal communication or by written memorandum. The memorandum is a time-saver and can provide identical, specific information to all its addressees, but it is rather abrupt and one-sided. At times it should be preceded by discussion sessions to prepare people for what is going to happen, allow them to ask questions and have their say about it. What they say may make worthwhile contributions and reveal unconsidered factors. Furthermore, successful production depends not only on tables of organization but on the spirit of cooperation between departments, which will be greater when they have a chance to participate in the production planning.

When launching a new program, therefore, it is profitable to hold a production conference, attended by such persons as the producer or sponsor's representative, producer-director, and delegates from Design and Graphics, Staging and Lighting, and Engineering. Topics may include deadlines, budget, style of the production, and what each department should and can provide for it.

Decisions of this conference can be confirmed by a "production requirements memo." Such a memorandum may also announce changes in the requirements of an existing program, as illustrated by Figure 1. Like other forms reproduced in this chapter, Figure 1 merely represents the practice of one station. Although all stations may not use the same forms, they are likely to have similar obligations. Thus, all of them need to inform their

FIG. 1

PRODUCTION REQUIREMENTS MEMO

Strunk (3)   Evans   Pedry   July 13, 1963
Carroll   Malone   Vance
Oberg   Newsome Schlater cc Finlayson
Cassman   Duffy   Banks   cc Schute

TRUMPETEERS COLORCAST

TIME: July 18, 2:00-3:00 pm

STUDIO: (this day only) D-1

CONTENT: Celebrating our new color cameras, this show will use a circus
theme and the following cast:

    Mayor Helmholz, to dedicate venture
    Walt Malone as ringmaster
    Sanford Sisters and Martin Malone, vocals
    Sandra Mae and Gene Johnson, dancers
    Roger Dubeck, magic as a sideshow barker
    Kerry Faith, vocal as a trapeze artist
    Carole Kailer, vocal as a gypsy fortune teller
    The Trumpeteers, as a circus band

DIRECTOR: Oberg

ENGINEERING: 1 color camera with electrazoom, 1 color camera with
normal lenses including 35mm. 1 boom mike with operator. Long fixed
boom from catwalk to cover band. Piano mike. Hand mike for ringmaster.

STAGING: Drapes, risers, folding chairs, & music racks as on floor plan.
Circus ring painted on floor. Trapeze for Kerry Faith. Draped table
& two chairs for fortune teller; cloth to cover 8-ball on this table.
Kraft model merry-go-round, blonde piano and piano bench (2-seater)
for Sanford Sisters. Costumes as previously discussed.

REHEARSAL SCHEDULE:

Friday evening, July 16		Sunday, July 18	
0700-0800	Cast: costumes, makeup	1130-1200	Cast: costumes, makeup
0800-1000	Band needed	1200 noon	Band report
0800-1030	Cameras needed	1200-0145	Fax rehearsal
		0200-0300	AIR

CHANGED STUDIOS FOR OTHER SHOWS:

To avoid interference with TRUMPETEERS, following shows will originate
this weekend only from Studio A-2:
Friday, July 16: HARPER COMMIS, 9:15 NEWS, 9:25 WEATHER
Sunday, July 18: SENTINEL COMICS

Contrary to previous advice, BLUE ROOM of July 16 and all shows
normally scheduled for D-1 on Saturday, July 17, will remain in D-1.

                                        Warren Beecher
                                        Production Manager

staffs about the conditions and requirements of each scheduled production: the names of its director, sponsor, producer, and staff announcer, the dates and times when facilities are needed, the basic facilities expected from each department, and the effect of the production on other station operations. (Even the receptionist may be affected if the "peanut gallery" is to be occupied daily by three troops of Boy Scouts who will eat box lunches in the lobby.)

SYSTEMATIZING THE PRODUCTION ACTIVITY

When the producer-director takes over, he will let the departments know his wants in more detail. These flats must be constructed. This film insert will be used. A bust of Beethoven must be found for the piano. Camera 2 will need the pedestal and the zoom lens. The montage amplifier must be working for those wipes. This is what we need lettered for the roll drum . . .

There must be some system for making these needs known and insuring that they are properly taken care of. Talking with the departments will serve only so far; they are busy with other projects; their memories may fail them; many of their people will need identical, specific information. The information should be recorded, quick to prepare, easy to understand. Hence there is a need for forms.

FIG. 2

FORMAT

HOUSE NEXT DOOR
12:45 – 12:59-30 PM

DAY _____

12:45:00	OPEN – SLIDES – THEME	:30
12:45:30	NELSON & GUEST	
	GUEST FEATURE #1 _____	
	_____	
	_____	
12:48:30	COMMERCIAL #1 _____	1:00
	NELSON & GUEST	
	GUEST FEATURE #2 _____	

Space will suffice to mention only a few of the forms which may be used to systematize production activity. Among these, of course, is the program script or format (see Figure 2), which serves to coordinate activities during rehearsal and performance. The station is likely to specify a particular script form so that information of specific kinds will be consistently and prominently displayed; thus the projectionist can readily see where slides and films occur, and the audio operator can spot microphone and music cues without searching.

It is likely that the station will have floor plans of its studios on which directors can diagram the placement of sets and equipment, using a standard scale and symbols that can be commonly and readily interpreted.

Directors may also be required to submit a sheet listing data about the music to be used on their programs, which is needed to ascertain whether the rights to perform it or record it are held by the station or can be secured. (Figure 3.)

There will also probably be some form of "work order" or "service request," such as shown in Figure 4. Useful for many purposes (getting properties constructed, title cards lettered, film shot), this form goes from the producer-director to the appropriate department, where it takes its place in the "to do" file in relation to orders of greater or lesser priority. Sometimes, to prevent unreasonable demands on the service departments, the order will require an authorizing signature from the administrator in charge of production. Having completed the job, the department may complete the form by recording the cost of materials and labor used,

FIG. 3

(Local Emanations Only) PROGRAM TITLE SPONSOR	MUSIC SHEET Dialogue:Yes__No__ Costumes:Yes__No__	Date Day From AM PM To AM PM

Title	Station File No.	Artist	Writer	Publisher	License Agent

FIG. 4

WORK ORDER OR SERVICE REQUEST

TO: Traffic & Continuity   FROM_____
    Film
    Design & Graphics   ORDER NO._____ DATE_____
    Staging   FOR PROGRAM_____
    Engineering   DEADLINE, DATE_____HOUR_____
    Other_____   CHARGE ACCOUNT #_____

DESCRIPTION OF REQUEST:

thus providing a basis for program cost accounting or for billing the program sponsor.

A special form of order is usually required for video tape recordings, playbacks, and erasures. (See Figure 5.) On the back of this example there is space to enter any deficiencies in performance or technical quality which will need to be kept in mind when the tape is broadcast.

If a station does much production outside its studios, it will need a "remote survey form" to serve as a record of the many arrangements which must be made regarding power supply, transmission lines, location of equipment, police permits, meals, transportation, and many other considerations. Figure 6 shows a sample page from one such form, which comprises four pages.

Any form is only as good as its deadline. Much of a production supervisor's time can be consumed in seeing that forms reach the departments concerned in time for them to fit the jobs entailed into their normal working patterns. This means time not only to accomplish these particular jobs, but also those for other programs which are in progress. Departments must be allowed ample opportunity to turn out work they can be proud of, and they should not be expected to give priority to one client at the expense of another.

The time of departments must be used efficiently, avoiding as much as possible the alleged army rhythm of "hurry up and wait." It is important to plan how their physical and human resources will be employed throughout every hour of the week. How long will Schmidt and Melby be needed on video control? When can they be

FIG. 5

FIG. 5

TO: TV Engineering (2)
    Director (2)
    Suspense File _____
                    (Date)

CODE NO. VT_____

Position_____

VIDEO TAPE RECORDING ORDER

Please video tape _____
                    (Name or description of production)

_____   _____
(Taping Date)   (Taping time - hour)

                                    Dry rehearsal_____

                                    Cam. rehearsal_____

_____   _____
(Studio or point of origin)   (Length of production)

_____   _____
(Name of director)   (Others involved, if required)

_____
(Name of producer)

For use as follows:

_____
        (Names ---- Day ---- Date ---- Time of telecast)

Comments or special instructions:
(SEE REVERSE SIDE)

                            Ordered by _____
                                            (Signature)

ERASE ORDER

(Tape not to be erased unless a positive, signed erase order is issued.)

This tape is to be erased after _____

                        Authorized by_____

FIG. 6

'Live___, CC___, VTR___, Sim___ REMOTE SURVEY FORM   (to be completed by director,
Mic. Wave___, Cable___, Van___   studio supervisor and
                                                        technical supervisor)

PROGRAM_____ SERIES_____
PRODUCER_____ DIRECTOR_____
DATE OF SURVEY_____TIME_____ PERMISSION TO SURVEY
                                                      GRANTED BY_____
CONTACT AT LOCATION_____ MADE BY_____
DATE OF FIRST PICKUP_____ LOCATION_____
                                 ADDRESS_____
OTHER PERMISSION: TO PARK MOBILE UNITS GRANTED BY_____
                  TO RUN LINES GRANTED BY_____

TIMES: SETUP MOBILE UNIT   DAY_____ TIME_____ MEETING PLACE_____
       SETUP MICROWAVE   DAY_____ TIME_____ MEETING PLACE_____
       REHEARSAL SCHEDULE DAY_____ CAMS_____ AIR_____RECORD_____

TECHNICAL SUPERVISOR_____APPROVED_____

CONTACTS

YES	NO	POSITION	NAME		PHONE
___	___	TELEPHONE REP.			PHONE____
___	___	HOUSE ELECTRICIAN			PHONE____
___	___	BUILDING MANAGER			PHONE____
___	___	POLICE DEPARTMENT			PHONE____
___	___	_____			PHONE____
___	___				PHONE____

NEAREST PHONE TO MOBILE UNIT_____PHONE____

TERMINATION POINTS AND EQUIPMENT LOCATIONS

YES	NO			CABLE	ft
___	___	POWER FOR MOBILE UNIT		CABLE	ft
___	___	POWER FOR MOBILE VTR		CABLE	ft
___	___	REMOTE SOUND AMPLIFIER		CABLE	ft
___	___	AUDIO LINES		CABLE	ft
___	___	TELEPHONE LINE		CABLE	ft
___	___	MICROWAVE XMTR		CABLE	ft
___	___	MICROWAVE RECEIVER		CABLE	ft
___	___	MOBILE UNIT (BUS)			
___	___	MOBILE VTR (VAN)		CABLE	ft
___	___	VIDEO MONITORS		CABLE	ft
___	___	OTHER		CABLE	ft
___	___	OTHER		CABLE	ft

CAMERAS   NEEDED #_____   PLACEMENT   LENSES MOUNT CABLE   ORTH

YES	NO		PLACEMENT	LENSES	MOUNT	CABLE	ORTH
___	___	NO. 1		___	___	___ft.	___
___	___	NO. 2		___	___	___ft.	___
___	___	NO. 3		___	___	___ft.	___
___	___	NO. 4		___	___	___ft.	___
___	___	CONSTRUCTION REQUIRED					

PERMISSION TO CONSTRUCT AND/OR LOCATE GRANTED BY_____

SOUND EQUIPMENT   PLACEMENT   TYPE   MOUNT CABLE

YES	NO		PLACEMENT	TYPE	MOUNT	CABLE
___	___	NO. 1		___	___	___ft
___	___	NO. 2		___	___	___ft
___	___	NO. 3		___	___	___ft
___	___	NO. 4		___	___	___ft
___	___	AMPEX 601		___	___	___ft
___	___	OTHER		___	___	___ft

used for maintenance? Must Rodjinski be brought in on overtime to finish the set construction, because he'll work all afternoon as floor director? When should the set-up for "Channel Chatter" be ready in Studio A? When will Studio B be free for installing those new outlets? What time will the late shift have to report next week?

In order to assign their equipment and personnel, the departments (particularly Staging Facilities and Engineering) need to know what production activity has been scheduled and when and where it is to take place. They learn this from the production supervisor's "studio schedule," "production schedule," or "crew time schedule," examples of which are shown in Figures 7, 8, and 9. Such schedules usually comprise a week's activity and are issued early enough for departments to make their assignments before the week begins.

As a study of Figure 8 will reveal, these schedules aim for as

FIG. 7

Monday, April 29, 1963   PRODUCTION SCHEDULE

PROGRAM TITLE	TYPE	STU	CAM	DRY FAX AIR	VTR#	TAPE#	POS	DIR	STU SUP
LAND OF PLAY	LIV	A	2	0830 0845 0930 0845 0930 1000				Shaw	Lnds
C'S CLUBHOUSE	VTR PB	T		1000 1030	60-32	118½	HT		

FIG. 8

STUDIO SCHEDULE, MONDAY, SEPTEMBER 9

REHEARSAL ROOM

0700-0745 Psych dry (Gale)

STUDIO 1

0345-0420 Totem dry
0420-0430 TOTEM FAX
0430-0500 TOTEM CLUB (Stsn) L

STUDIO 2

0130-0200 Phys Sci dry
0200-0230 Humanities dry
0230-0245 HUMANITIES FAX
0245-0300 PHYS SCI FAX
0300-0330 PHYS SCI (Forsberg) L-VTR
0330-0400 HUMANITIES (Gale) L-VTR

0500-0520 Accounting dry

Fig. 9

Mr. Leeser	(2)	Miss Jones	Mr. Wallace	Mr. Lemonds
Mr. Petrie	(2)	Mr. McCormack	Mr. Browender	Mr. Preuss
Mr. Birmingham	(2)	Mr. Skowronski	Miss Beimer	Mr. McGrath
Mr. Reth	(3)	Mr. Thomas	Miss Tarantino	Mr Steele

Muscians' Lounge B.B.

April 25, 1963

CREW TIME, MAY 6, 1963 – MAY 12, 1963
MONDAY, MAY 6, 1963

STUDIO M/A (Control thru Master)

7:15 – 7:25	Fax Ch	1	1 ped
7:25 – 7:30	TODAY—MILWAUKEE NEWS	1	1 ped
8:25 – 8:30	TODAY—MILWAUKEE NEWS	1	1 ped
3:45 – 3:55	Fax Ch	1	1 ped
4:00 – 5:40	THEATRE AT FOUR	1	1 ped

STUDIO D/A

8:15 – 8:25	TFW Fax Ch	4	3 peds
8:30 – 8:55	TFW Rhsl	4	3 peds
9:00 – 10:00	TODAY FOR WOMEN	4	3 peds

STUDIO D-1

11:30 – 11:45	Kids/News/Wthr/Colnik Rhsl	5	2 chromas
11:45 – 11:55	Fax Ch	5	2 chromas
12:00 – 12:30	KIDS KLUB	5	2 chromas
12:30 – 12:45	WTHR/NEWS	5	2 chromas
12:45 – 1:00	COLNIK	5	2 chromas
5:30 – 5:40	Fax Ch	4	2 peds
5:40 – 5:55	S/N/W & S.A. Rhsl	4	2 peds
6:00 – 6:30	S/N/W & S.A.	4	2 peds
9:15 – 9:25	Fax Ch	5	2 chromas
9:30 – 9:45	News/Wthr Rhsl	5	2 chromas
9:45 – 9:55	Fax Ch	5	2 chromas
10:00 – 10:30	WTHR/NEWS/SPORTS	5	2 chromas

STUDIO D-1 (VT Session)

10:00 – 10:05	TFW PROMO (VT)	4	2 peds
11:05 – 11:15	Fax Ch	3	1 chroma
11:15 – 11:30	EDITORIALS (VT) (COLOR)	3	1 chroma
1:00 – 1:10	KIDS KLUB & MIDDAY PROMOS (VT)	4	1 chroma
3:00 – 3:10	Fax Ch	4	2 peds
3:15 – 4:00	SUN NITE THEATRE (VT)	4	2 peds
7:15 – 7:25	Fax Ch	4	2 peds
7:30 – 8:30	TFW FEATURE (VT)	4	2 peds
	(St. Peters Lutheran School operetta)		
9:10 – 9:25	NEWS ROUNDUP FEATURES (VT)	2	D Control Audio/Video
10:30 – 10:40	Fax Ch	3	1 ped
10:45 – 10:55	MIDNIGHT NEWS (VT)	3	1 ped

STUDIO D/A (VT Session)

1:30 – 1:40	Breaks Fax Ch	4	1 ped
1:45 – 2:45	BREAKS (VT)	4	1 ped
4:00 – 4:10	Judy Promos Fax Ch	4	1 ped
4:10 – 4:30	JUDY PROMOS (VT)	4	1 ped

much efficiency as possible. Since "Phys Sci" and "Humanties" are broadcast in immediate succession, the "fax" (facilities check) for both programs must be made before the first one begins. Instead of scheduling these checks in the same order as the programs, that for the first program has been scheduled last so that cameras will not have to move to the "Humanities" set just before air time. While these programs are in progress, the crew that set their scenery and lighting can move over to Studio 1 to set "Totem Club"; and because the program manager has scheduled a recorded program between 4:00 and 4:30, there is time for the engineers who worked in Studio 2 to shut down their equipment there and be ready by 4:20 for the "Totem fax" in Studio 1. Meanwhile, the stagehands move into Studio 2 to strike "Phys Sci" and "Humanities" and have "Accounting" set and lighted by 5:00, when its dry rehearsal begins.

Video tape recording can make a special contribution to the efficient scheduling of production activity, since programs to be aired over the weekend can be recorded between Monday and Friday and programs scheduled for evening broadcast can be recorded by the daytime crew, minimizing needs for an evening shift.

Efficiency comes, of course, not only from schedules and forms, but from finding the best way to do things; and so that these best ways may be formalized, there is a periodic need for the production management to issue certain policy statements and regulations. For example, there will probably be a set of studio regulations:

> Please . . .
> Use the sound lock when the red light is on.
> Avoid stepping on cables.
> Leave personal belongings in dressing rooms, not on studio equipment.
> Close the doors to keep cool air in and noises out.

—and whatever else is necessary to promote studio efficiency.

In the interest of efficient relations between departments, the person in charge of production will keep in close touch with other staff administrators, which may require no effort since they are sure to seek him out with various complaints. "Look," says the chief engineer, "I scheduled my cameramen for 7:30 last night like you said, and your director kept on dry rehearsing until 7:47!" or, "The union steward says he saw your floor director move a camera during the 'News' set-up," or, "You can't expect my men to go on that remote at 8 A.M. when they work the night before till 11:30!"

CONTROLLING THE QUALITY OF PRODUCTION

The chief engineer will probably also point out how production people have lowered the quality of the pictures taken by his cameras. "Why didn't we get to see that film insert before it went on 'Sports Parade' today? Parts of it had so much density we couldn't shade it up to make out anything! And by the way, your director kept the cameras right up to air time and didn't give us a chance to balance them. And say, when are you going to get that news commentator to stop wearing white shirts with dark blue suits?"

He's right, of course. Good television picture quality depends just as much on production people as on engineers. Production management, therefore, can involve a constant effort to educate lighting and staging people, directors and performers to the requirements of the electronic system and the engineers who operate it. On the other hand, it may sometimes attempt to educate engineers to the creative and expressive concerns of production people. Not always does a director want an even focus on every element in the picture, nor does he want all the faint and loud passages in the music potted to sound like the rest of the composition. The goal, of course, is that engineering and production understand each other's problems and work to achieve quality together.

The control of production quality involves other concerns than engineering, however, and it may very well begin before a program has been accepted for production. Each program proposal should be assessed not only for its value to a sponsor and an audience, but also for its production potentialities. It is sometimes not as obvious as it should be that an idea for a program is not a program. Before committing an important venture to broadcast, it may be prudent to inspect not only a sample script but even a pilot performance.

At least, the idea should be scrutinized in terms of the station's ability to manufacture the product. Most industrial manufacturing processes have certain controls to insure that their products measure up to standards. Although (or perhaps because) television production works with human beings, controls for human variables are just as (or even more) important. Among possible television controls are:

The known abilities of performers and of the production personnel.

The amount of rehearsal available.

The provision that amateur performers will not be expected to deliver more than seems comfortable and familiar to them.

The possibility of developing a basic routine of proven effectiveness which can become "second nature" to the people who execute it.

In ad-libbed situations, the existence of a clear plan of action, with responsibility centralized in one person who is capable of keeping the program moving, and moving in the right direction.

Before starting a production venture, many questions should be asked: Are the right performers available? Are other materials available; and if they belong to others, can permission to use them be secured? How much camera rehearsal does the program require? How much studio space? What studio utilities (gas, water, 220v electric power)? What special facilities and effects? Is the idea suited to the space and time continuum of live television shooting, or does it require the greater flexibility of film technique? If a series is proposed, are its individual programs sufficiently alike in format and staging conditions so that what has been learned by producing the first may be transferred to producing the others, or does each require a fresh start and a new solution? What about costs—for talent, clearance of rights, rental of special equipment, construction, transportation, film stock and processing, etc.? Is there enough budget to produce this program as it ought to be produced? And if the program proposal comes from outside the station, do sponsor and station see eye-to-eye on its purpose and treatment?

Although it is doubtless not proper for a production supervisor to tell a program manager his business, it sometimes happens, particularly in the area of educational and public service programming, that a producer-director is handed a program which it is almost impossible to bring to any satisfactory state of life and interest. Hence these further questions: Why will this proposal make a good television program (rather than, say, a literary work)? What is alive about it? What action occurs? What is there to watch and listen to? Why will it interest its intended audience? What appeals are inherent in its

subject matter (timeliness; satisfaction of human pleasures, desires, needs, etc.)?

ingredients (qualities of its performers, scenic environment, visuals, films, etc.)?

construction (variety, pace, coherence, climax, suspense, conflict, etc.)?

When such appeals exist, the producer-director will find it easier to do an effective job.

Certainly the production management must assign a producer-director who is sympathetic with the program style and content; and the station's "stable" of producer-directors should provide a range from which to choose; a man qualified to handle sports is not necessarily good at art and music programs, and vice versa.

Once a director has been assigned, he should not be left entirely to his own devices. Someone should be available either to restrain or encourage him, as circumstances dictate. The restraint may be necessary if his imagination escapes the bounds of mature judgment or if his enthusiastic involvement with a single program leads him to demand resources which are needed concurrently by other programs or which are beyond the capabilities of the station to supply or afford. More often, however, he needs the encouragement of someone who will consult with him about his problems and help to solve them. In some stations a producer-director can be frustrated by departments which put their own convenience before the needs of the programs which they are supposed to serve.

A good production supervisor will try to prevent this condition and promote an enthusiastic spirit of participation on the part of all departments, leading them to declare, "If this will make the program better, let's try it, let's do it!" And when they *do* do it, it will help to perpetuate their spirit if they are congratulated on the results. Thus they are led to feel that it is *their* program, too.

Helping the producer-director includes monitoring his broadcasts from time to time and making suggestions for their improvement. This requires not that the supervisor carp and spy, but that he encourage his personnel through evident interest in the development of their abilities, meanwhile setting an example by his own ability in production skills and judgments. Ideally, he should be able to contribute to the growth of his people by sharpening their sense of showmanship and increasing the communicative values of their camerawork.

No matter how hard everyone strives to maintain the quality of production, occasional troubles are bound to occur. It is an obligation of production management to find out about these troubles promptly and take immediate steps to correct them. Some stations require the producer-director to file a trouble report in writing immediately after the duty shift during which the trouble occurred. Sometimes the trouble will result from equipment failure, sometimes from human error. Sometimes the "buck" will be passed between two persons or two departments. This calls for a willingness to seek out and listen to both sides of the case with as much judiciousness as possible.

Improving production quality also depends upon improving the physical means of production, keeping abreast of what is new and better in the line of studio facilities, shop tools, camera accessories, switching devices, and other equipment. Sometimes the person in charge of production will himself recommend such improvements; sometimes they will be urged on him by his assistants. If they are engineering devices, he must try to convince the chief engineer of their worth. And in any case, he must measure their worth as improvements against the financial cost of acquiring them.

CONTROLLING THE COSTS OF PRODUCTION

Financial costs are a matter of concern to the manager of production in any kind of station, for commercial stations need to make money, and educational stations need to make money go as far as possible. A knowledge of costs is essential, both to keep the production operation within its budget and to have a basis on which to assess charges to clients.

One of the first questions likely to be asked about a proposed production is, "How much will it cost?" To answer, one must be able to estimate the production requirements in terms of space and time, of labor, materials, equipment, and administrative overhead. Then one applies predetermined rates: so much per hour per single camera chain, per zoomar lens, per video tape machine used to record, per director, per studio with basic facilities and minimum crew; so much per unit for processed 2" x 2" slides or lettered title cards. (See the estimate sheet reproduced as Figure 10.)

Determining these rates may involve a knowledge of many different cost factors. The rate for video recording, for example, may take into consideration: (1) the average hourly wage for video tape operators; (2) depreciation of the recording heads, which must be renewed after a certain number of hours of use; (3) the initial price of the recorder and associated equipment, depreciated over a certain number of years of useful life; (4) a percentage which experience has shown to represent the cost of labor, maintenance equipment, replacement parts, and electrical power needed to operate and maintain the machine. Then, either built into each separate rate or added to the total of all services billed or estimated, there must be a percentage to cover overhead—the cost of clerical and administrative services and of the station premises, including their upkeep, heat, light, and other utilities. For billing, of course, another factor should be added for profit.

Although accounts receivable will doubtless be kept by the station business manager, this manager will be told by the supervisor of production what to bill for production supplies and services. As already noted, he may receive some of this information on copies of completed work orders. Also from the production supervisor he will receive instructions about talent payments and payments for overtime accrued by production personnel.

Negotiation of talent fees may be the responsibility of each producer-director, who is then expected to report these fees to his supervisor, possibly for approval before the talent is actually hired, although in many instances the producer-director is given free rein

FIG. 10

WMSB TELEVISION
CHANNEL 10

Date:_____

ESTIMATE OF FACILITIES RENTAL AND PERSONNEL COSTS

ESTIMATED COST	HOURS	RATE	QUANTITY	ITEM	ACTUAL COST
$_____	_____	_____	_____	Studio w/o Facilities	_____
$_____	_____	_____	_____	Studio & Facilities	_____
$_____	_____	_____	_____	Master Control Facilities	_____
$_____	_____	_____	_____	Projection Facilities	_____
$_____	_____	_____	_____	Remote Unit-Empty	_____
$_____	_____	_____	_____	Remote Unit-Equipped	_____
$_____	_____	_____	_____	Microwave Unit	_____
$_____	_____	_____	_____	GPL Watson Electric	_____
				Zoomar Lens	
$_____	_____	_____	_____	Single Camera Chain	_____
$_____	_____	_____	_____	Videotape Recorder-Record	_____
$_____	_____	_____	_____	Videotape Preview Playback	_____
$_____	_____	_____	_____	Videotape Sale	_____
$_____	_____	_____	_____	Videotape Rental	_____
$_____	_____	_____	_____	Videotape Editing	_____
$_____	_____	_____	_____	Kinescope Recorder	_____
$_____	_____	_____	_____	Kinescope Editing	_____
$_____	_____	_____	_____	Director &/or Producer	_____
$_____	_____	_____	_____	Production Personnel	_____
$_____	_____	_____	_____	Engineering Personnel	_____
$_____	_____	_____	_____	Student Labor	_____
$_____	_____	_____	_____	Photographic Costs*	_____
$_____	_____	_____	_____	Properties	_____
$_____	_____	_____	_____	Sets	_____
$_____	_____	_____	_____	TOTAL	_____
$_____	_____	_____	_____	Administrative Overhead	_____
$_____	_____	_____	_____	TOTAL (Inc. Overhead)	$_____

SIGNED_____
     Robert D. Page
     Production & Facilities Manager

*Cost breakdown on separate sheet.

Note--A complete description of the above
    items is available on request.

to spend what he considers necessary, providing that he keeps within his budget.

NEGOTIATIONS

There are certain major negotiations, however, which affect the station as a whole rather than a single program and must consequently be a function of production management. These may include contractual negotiations with performers', musicians', and stagehands' unions, and licensing agreements with firms which control the rights to music and other copyrighted materials which the station wishes to use in its productions.

Even if he has not personally conducted such negotiations, it is essential that the production supervisor be intimately familiar with their terms, since they affect what can be done and what cannot be done—or what can be done only by paying a premium price. Furthermore, he should see that the producer-directors also know and observe these terms, just as he should see that they know and observe the regulations of the Federal Communications Commission, the laws of copyright, libel, slander, and invasion of privacy, and any other station policies, ignorance of which will result in trouble.

Another class of negotiations may fall within the scope of production management. Sometimes a producer-director will need the support of higher authority to obtain rights, supplies, or services which require the permission of some high official. Will the museum allow some of its valuable exhibits to be brought to the studio? Can the outdoor swimming pool in City Park be used for the series on water safety? Can the pool be filled for this purpose when citizens are being restricted from watering their lawns because of a summer water shortage? Will the aeronautics authority allow a helicopter to land in the outdoor studio?

Occasionally an objection to such requests will come from an unforeseen direction. In the case of the helicopter landing, for instance, the local traffic authority may point out that it also should have been consulted lest gawking motorists cause a hazard on the busy highway adjoining the outdoor studio. When planning remote broadcasts (or any other new productions, for that matter), one must have enough imagination to foresee the unforeseeable.

SUMMARY

What other qualities one needs can best be appreciated after a brief review of what this chapter has established as the sphere of production management. What has been said amounts to this—that one or more persons in central positions of authority should do these things:

> Systematize the production process, coordinating its flow of supplies and services.
> Maintain and, where possible, improve the quality of production.
> Control the costs of production.
> Obtain rights and services which must be negotiated on a high administrative level.

Sometimes the station manager himself may participate in aspects of this activity. Sometimes the program manager will conduct the major part of it, with the production manager as his assistant. Sometimes the production manager, fulfilling all of the implications of his title, will be responsible for everything. If he is, he will need the following qualities:

> A knack for organization and pre-planning.
> An ability to deal successfully with people.
> A respect for economy.
> A knowledge of all of the creative and technical aspects of the production process.

CHAPTER 10

The News Department

BY JAY CROUSE

WHAS-TV, Louisville, Kentucky

A graduate of the University of Missouri School of Journalism, Mr. Crouse began his career with the *Cincinnati Post*. The recipient of numerous awards, including the Distinguished Reporting Award of the Louisville Professional Chapter of Sigma Delta Chi, national journalism society, he is now News Director of WHAS-TV-Radio in Louisville, Kentucky.

THE role of broadcast news is the same as printed news—to inform the public. This is journalism, and trained journalists must do the job. Basically the only difference between the newspaper reporter and the electronic journalist is equipment. Both deal in facts. Both weave these facts into a report, or story. Both communicate this finished product, the story, to the general public. We in electronic journalism have a distinct advantage over our newspaper colleagues. Our facts are fleshed out with the sight and sound of the story, which breathes life into our reports. The television viewer not only hears what we are talking about, he sees the story developing as we sketch it for him.

This type of reporting really is not so excitingly new that it can't be easily defined. It is basic communication. And it demands that the practitioners be good reporters first. Electronic journalism today, and even more so in the future, needs qualified, competent newsmen. The plain fact is that our business is constantly changing due to improved equipment and techniques. It takes a knowledgeable man just to keep pace with the constantly changing methods, but a trained and capable reporter or news writer can always find a good slot in a television newsroom.

THE TELEVISION NEWSROOM

What is a television newsroom? Take the average city room of a daily newspaper. Maintain the same general area to be covered. Slash the reportorial staff in half. Cut the half down the middle again so that one ends up with about one fourth the manpower of the newspaper city room. This manpower requirement represents the ideal. From a practical standpoint most newsrooms are short staffed. Add all the necessary wires, microphones, cameras, cables, tubes, transistors and other paraphernalia required for the transmission of picture and sound. Don't overlook the newsman's basic tools: pencils and paper, telephones, typewriters, sturdy legs and what may well be a sixth sense, an innate judgment called "a nose for news." Don't overlook the wire services, the still and film syndication services and the development of an organized and efficiently operating stringer system. Then there is the library or morgue set-up—nothing more than a good filing system. Remember the organization is a functioning unit seven days a week, day and night. The sum total is, at best, organized confusion. At worst, utter chaos. But order can and must be brought about.

The starting place lies with station management. The general manager must have an awareness of what his television newsroom is, and what it can do for him; what it is from the standpoint of what its needs and requirements are; what it can do for him from the angle of the station's over-all image to the general public. First and foremost, the newsroom must be a separate department. The news director must be responsible only to the station manager. This is not to say that the newsroom is an independent entity. Certainly it is only one department of the over-all operation of a television station. There is some overlapping between news and, say, programming; between news and continuity*; between news and production. But where this intertwining occurs, the newsroom must retain complete responsibility for the content of news shows. Station management must be fully aware that the News Department is not, can not and should not be considered as merely another revenue

---

* "Continuity is a word from radio which describes the transitions between the segments of any type of program. Occasionally, this word may be used to mean the *script* or *commercial* itself," is the definition given in *Television Production: The TV Handbook and Dictionary* by Harry Wayne McMahan (Hastings House, 1957) —Ed.

producer. Some News Departments do operate at a profit. More often than not, they incur an operating deficit. But remember, news is a service to the public. When that public develops a healthy respect for the news operation, the station image takes a giant stride forward. And an efficient, worthwhile news operation cannot be predicated upon dollars and cents alone. It can and must be developed from the understanding and upon the framework that trained journalists are required to do the job.

These reporters, or newsmen, must have the freedom to practice their craft. There must be a direct line of communication between the station management and the news director. The news director must be on an equal basis with all other department heads in the operation. When programming, engineering, production or some other department begins to have a say in the day-to-day operation of the newsroom, the role of the broadcast journalist becomes secondary. The public will not get the information it requires. Only when a station manager buys this basic premise, that his news director is responsible solely to him, can he take the first step toward molding an efficient, capable news operation.

Of course, a corollary exists here. Newspeople must perform their jobs to the utmost of their ability. And then strain a bit to do their job just that much better. Every day. Day in and day out. Not just on the big, breaking stories.

The image of the station in its market is closely connected with the news job it does. The news director and his newsmen are probably better known than the sales manager or even the station manager at most civic functions. The news director or his reporters are the ones who come into daily contact with the lifelines of the community. The News Department is the one department of the station that has the opportunity to portray the station to the public every day.

THE NEWS DIRECTOR'S CREDO

This commitment to news is perhaps best outlined in the following credo of the Radio Television News Directors Association:

> The Radio Television News Directors Association believes that the broadcasting of factual, objective and timely news is the finest public service radio or television stations can perform. An

important objective for which every radio and television station should strive is a newsroom competently staffed and honestly operated, with every effort made to give its listeners and viewers complete, prompt and intelligently-screened newscasts.

In the furtherance of this belief and this objective, RTNDA subscribes its allegiance to these "Standards of Practice." Furthermore, RTNDA insists on the compliance of its members with the "Standards of Practice."

STANDARDS OF PRACTICE

1) The news director, as a key figure in the broadcasting industry, has the public interest as his foremost responsibility. His principal purpose is to keep the public well-informed.

2) Complete coverage of the news is the news director's prime objective, and the emphasis should be on scope and understanding, particularly as it concerns the news within his own listening area.

3) Material selected for newscasts must be judged on its news merit alone.

4) News presentation must be accurate, factual, in good taste, and without bias. Writer and newscaster should co-operate to avoid sensationalism in reporting, writing, editing and broadcasting.

5) The use of the word "Bulletin" should be limited to label only those reports of such transcendent interest that they warrant interrupting the regular broadcasting schedule. The word "Flash" must not be used contrary to its historic meaning in news usage.

6) Commentary and analysis must be clearly identified in all news broadcasts.

7) Editorial material must not be mixed with factual news reporting, and when it is used, it must be clearly labeled.

8) The race, creed, color or previous status of an individual in the news should not be mentioned unless it is necessary to the understanding of the story.

9) No story, either wire copy or locally written, should be used until the newscaster has read it understandingly. The only acceptable exception would be a late-breaking story of such importance that the news director or the newsman on duty considers it a "must" for a news program already on the air.

THE PROFESSION OF BROADCAST JOURNALISM

The extent and diversity of techniques in television make broadcast journalism a profession encompassing varied and highly specialized services. One could be a film editor, a producer of news documentaries, an investigative reporter, a beat man, a news commentator, a correspondent for the national networks or a large chain of stations, a newsfilm cameraman, an editorial research specialist, or a news editor blending the national, international and local news for an up-to-the minute news report. This brief list of specialized jobs in broadcast journalism could go on, but the fact of the matter is that a television newsman more than likely will be a combination of some, or all, of these. However, all of these talents and skills will be built on the foundation of all journalism: the gathering, writing and reporting of the news.

There is a shortage of trained and competent radio and television newsmen. There are job openings for qualified people in every state, but the emphasis is on trained, competent journalists.

When the new recruit walks into the average television newsroom, eager and ready to tackle his first assignment, he's looking for experience. He's also ready to put his training and ideals to the test. In reality, it is a testing period both for the recruit and for the newsroom. Some never make it. Some adapt as easily as the proverbial duck taking to water. Most at least face the initial disenchantment of learning that he steps onto the bottom rung of the ladder at 3:30 in the morning.

If the embryonic Edward R. Murrow possesses a sense of personal dedication, displays maturity, offers good judgment and demonstrates resourcefulness, he'll make it hands down. Paul White, the founder and former director of News and Public Affairs for the Columbia Broadcasting System, had a somewhat longer list of qualifications. His list included: integrity, curiosity, energy, good health, intelligence, objectivity, resourcefulness—even the qualification of being "able to survive innumerable toasts at a Russian Banquet." One could quarrel with none of these—except to point out, of course, that the novice newsman ought not to rush out for a speedy course in Russian at the nearest Berlitz school—nor should he stock up on vodka and caviar for the time being. It may be some time before his beat includes international conferences. In broadcast jour-

nalism, there is, however, one quality that stands out. That's dedica-·
tion. It's a quality that's associated with all professions: the desire
to serve others. Make no mistake about it, broadcast journalism is
a profession.

There are too many news-oriented people today who still view
news as being conducted only from the working end of a microphone or camera. Once they find out that more often than not it
takes them away from the "glamour side" of the business, they're
ready to run to the nearest program director with their idea of what
a disc jockey show ought to sound like, or they'll try to palm off
their meager talents as a sports man as the quickest way to fame
and fortune.

Starting at, or near, the bottom in a television newsroom does
not mean that the newcomer will not be a member of the team. It
does mean that certain onerous tasks, which at the time may seem
to be totally insignificant, will fall to him. There is a certain amount
of drudgery, even in the fascinating field of journalism, that requires attention.

It is well to point out that some members of the "newsroom
team" are working in almost complete solitude, while others in
this "work-a-day" world have time off. Furthermore, the television
newsroom is a functioning operation, seven days a week, day and
night. Consequently, someone has to man the newsroom on week-
ends, late at night and early in the morning. The teletypes have to
be fed their daily increment of paper. The machines must have
ribbons replenished. The telephones have to be answered. Irate
listeners will make known their complaints, and courtesy is still the
best policy when dealing with an aroused citizen. The whole point
here is that news is not a game—but it definitely is fun, if one has
the right approach. It might be best to remember that the tedious
tasks serve as good discipline for the arduous work that lies ahead.

THE SCHEDULED NEWSCAST, LOCAL NEWS

The basic ingredient of the newsroom diet is the regularly scheduled newscast. These occur at regular intervals throughout the
day and consume a large portion of the newsroom's time and attention. Gathering the material to insert in these timely reports
occupies the time of all members of the newsroom team. Whether
a man is assigned basically to re-write or is out on the beat, his pri-

mary concern is the development of news contacts so his newsroom is aware of what is going to happen in his locality.

The tempo of the newsroom operation swings into high gear when the crew is working on an in-depth report or a special documentary. Television newsrooms are waking up to the fact that investigative reporting is their meat. This calls for newsmen: reporters who know how to dig for facts and assemble these nuggets of news into a gold mine of information.

The backbone of any television newsroom has to be its local news set-up. In addition to the beat men and local staff of cameramen who cover the area, the "stringer" system has been found to be very productive. By this method, the station can expand the news coverage of its area without adding full time staff members. The stringer system for film and voice reports operates substantially the way newspaper and magazine stringers do. The news director should set up the system and determine, by pre-arrangement with each stringer, the method of payment. Generally, the station furnishes the film and processing, and pays the stringer for each assignment. The stringer may send in stories on speculation, and payment will be based on usage of the story. In all cases, the stringer should be paid for any expenses incurred in obtaining the story.

The average bread winner may be able to operate without a budget, but the average newsroom cannot. Budgets, as a rule, are made to be broken. But generally, the best means of budgeting for a newsroom operation is the "before and after" method. The calendar year may be split into as many divisions as the Accounting Department deems feasible. The news director can look ahead to the coming period and budget whatever expenses he deems necessary to provide adequate coverage of the coming events. Then, after that period has been entered in the company's ledger sheets, and the actual expenses have been itemized, the news director can explain the differences between his earlier estimates and actual costs.

Wire Services and Film Services

The wire service chosen for your television newsroom is largely a matter of personal selection. Associated Press or United Press International offers its own particular advantages. The final choice will be dictated largely by the type of job each service does in a particular area, but the "A" wire or trunk wire of the service chosen is mandatory. Since the bulk of the newscasts are to be re-written, the depth of the material furnished by the newspaper wire is a vital necessity. Add to this the regional TTS (teletype setter wires) and the radio wire of the service selected. The radio wire is a valuable aid for other than news programming, as it furnishes stock market reports, farm market reports, informational features and sidebar material. For those stations who do not have access to their own or a newspaper picture morgue, the addition of fac-simile photoservice is a distinct asset.

The syndicated film service offered by the network to which a station is affiliated should also be investigated, although for the most part, the nets have yet to make these as attractive as they ought to be. Again, cost will be the determining factor, and it is better all around to invest money first in establishing a local film operation, so that daily newsreel is a mainstay of the news opera-tion. This has to come first, and the only reason it has not been given more prominence or emphasis here is because daily film operation on a local level by television newsrooms has got to be treated as an accepted fact of life.

Job Requirements

Now, what are the requirements for anyone interested in becoming a part of a television newsroom? Nothing too strenuous or demand-ing, really. A college degree, as in most business today, is almost a must. In our business, however, an equivalent amount of experi-ence in the field is a strong recommendation to the man who is do-ing the hiring. At the same time, it should be noted that in the broadcast news business, as in most other enterprises, the college graduate can be trained or molded quickly into a functioning cog in the newsroom team, while an old hand or experienced veteran may take longer to assimilate into the unit due to predetermined work habits. In any case, desire, dedication, and determination are perhaps the three most important qualities that can result in a use-ful and rewarding career in broadcast news.

CHAPTER 11

Advertising, Promotion and Publicity

BY HOWARD W. COLEMAN

WTCN-TV, Minneapolis-St. Paul, Minnesota

A graduate of Northwestern University, Mr. Coleman also holds a Master's degree in education and was a high school instructor for four years. He entered broadcasting as a publicity writer for NBC, Chicago, in the days of Dave Garroway, *Ding Dong School*, and *Kukla, Fran and Ollie*, later becoming Advertising and Promotion Manager for NBC's WNBQ-TV. Mr. Coleman has also been Assistant to the President of WJIM-TV-Radio in Lansing, Michigan, and is now Promotion Director for WTCN-TV-Radio in Minneapolis-St. Paul, owned by Time-Life Broadcast, Inc.

SOMEWHERE, in virtually every commercial television station in the land, there is a door or a desk with the label "Promotion" above, around or near it.

The physical locations vary widely—quite near the general manager, in a corner of the news department, or adjacent to the coffee machine or the men's room.

The decor most likely is early Grand Rapids gone to seed—a chair inherited when the sales manager's office was redone, a desk from a 1952 furniture commercial (never reclaimed by the client), a dog-eared 1940 unabridged dictionary on a wobbly mahogany stand.

Brass-painted ashtrays, pencil holders and rulers from *TV Guide* are standard, as are tall and well-filled utility wastebaskets. Cork bulletin boards cover much of the wall space: pinned, tacked, stapled and Scotch-taped to the boards are samples-samples-samples —newspaper ads, window streamers, "got-to-remember-this" memos, telegrams, movie lists, photos, bus cards, and at least ten other items that defy categorization.

The desk tops may most delicately be described as *messy*, the "in" baskets overflowing, the painted-brass ashtrays as well-filled as the wastebaskets, and the telephones well-worn.

In corners, and sometimes in the middle of the room as well, cardboard cartons rest in slightly dusty prominence—waiting the day "when nothing is happening" to be sorted or mailed or put in the basement. But the phones ring, and the typewriters clang, and a multitude of souls with important problems goes in and out—and the cartons sometimes pass from one promotion manager to the next without attention.

This is "Promotion"—source of prizes for the employees' club picnic, origination point of countless small invoices for inexplicable small items (as viewed by the business manager), non-revenue-producing budget load for the station manager, wailing wall for under-rated talent, provider of tickets and arranger of parties, whipping boy for the salesman who missed the sale, inevitable recipient of all phone calls that begin "Listen, you slobs, I want to tell you . . ."

Yes, this is promotion; or, punctuated in the eyebrow-raised viewpoint of visiting brass from the home office, *this* is promotion?

Promotion is many things indeed: newspaper advertising and contests, on-the-air production spots and fan magazine tune-in ads, rate card formats and mastheads for press releases, holiday parties and dump displays in supermarkets, night letters to "key buyers" and filler items to columnists . . .

The man—or sometimes woman—in charge of this area of station activity is invariably known as the *promotion manager*, even though many title-conscious ownerships may burnish the nameplate with *director of promotion* or better. In the NBC hierarchy, I once carried a business card that identified me as *director of advertising, promotion, merchandising and publicity*—actually a reasonably accurate, and certainly a resounding, cognomen. But alas, I was introduced to all and sundry as "our promotion man," and the general manager—originally a program man and slightly suspicious of all other departments—usually added as the ultimate accolade: "And he's not a bad sonofagun for his type!"

The professional promotion manager is in truth more than

anything else an *advertising* specialist—advertising the wares of his employer to several important groups.

He first of all advertises the output of his station to the public, to catch its interest and cause it to tune to his channel.

At the same time he advertises the efficacy of these wares—their ability to reach and to hold a mass audience, and to sell products—to advertising agencies and to clients.

Where practicable, and to a lesser degree, he advertises to the wholesalers, jobbers, brokers and retailers in the channels of mass merchandising the fact that one or another client is using his station's facilities to pre-sell the public on the superiority of one or another product.

Up to this point, our broadcast promotion manager is the exact counterpart of J. B. Snodgrass, who does this as advertising manager for Triple-A Nuts & Bolts, Inc., or a hundred other manufacturing outlets in any major market.

But the multiplicity of techniques, and the activities that range from blowing up balloons at a kiddy show remote telecast to determining the proper positioning of the foreign and domestic flags on the Cadillac when a visiting ambassador comes to town, make the term *advertising* seem tame.

And this same conglomoration of antic activities has a fatal attraction that makes J.B.'s nuts-and-bolts responsibilities appear as child's play to the working promoter!

With this introduction to promotion, it may well be time to get down to the Triple-A nuts-and-bolts of *television* promotion. Its responsibilities, as sketched out in brief above, are fairly simple in definition, and fall into certain over-all areas.

AUDIENCE PROMOTION

It is the most obvious of aphorisms to note that in commercial TV the program is only as good as the number of people who view it.

While the jaded promotion manager may sometimes come back with a much older saw that "you can drive a horse to water but you can't make him drink," it is nevertheless one of his most important, and quite possibly *the* most important, duties, to utilize every possible device to call the public's attention to his station.

As a disciple of the TV medium, he must first of all consider the possible uses of his own channel for this purpose. For each and every program, promotion kits provide promo spot copy in varying lengths, plus glossy photos, art, slides, sound-on-film trailers, and a variety of information pieces and feature material.

Beyond the normal routine of placing promotion material on the air in unused commercial time, he must push these materials in live programs, in other shows of similar audience appeal, in news or weather or sports programs, or in any other period on his station where the information can reach viewers favorably.

A budget for newspaper advertising is important, and should be a sizeable one. Outside of the network-owned-station markets, and in the top 30-to-50 market areas, the networks may split the cost of newspaper advertising on a 50-50 basis during the "premiere" net program introduction period in the fall. The wise promotion manager budgets to add his own tune-in advertising for key local programs; dominates the TV listings page during these September-October periods as a result.

During key rating periods throughout the season, he repeats with tune-in advertising of a similar theme and style, to continue to catch the public's eye. And he has up his sleeve at all times advertising layouts for the 52-week interview shows, kiddy programs, and news-weather-sports periods that are the staples of his station.

Fan magazines are an important additional source of audience promotion; *TV Guide,* present in regional editions in a major share of TV markets, trades space for station break spots as a matter of long-range policy. *How* the promotion man uses this space can be of major importance.

In addition, many of the larger markets have independent fan books similar to *Guide,* and many newspapers have weekly supplements in the same format. Time-space trades are general, and can be valuable adjuncts in program promotion.

Suburban newspapers (weekly, usually Thursday) are receptive to trading newspaper space for television time, recognizing that they can profit from TV advertising and that they are not in direct media competition. Major space (quarter- and half-pages) can usually be arranged with these groups; in addition to effective advertising, the proof sheets are invaluable in submitting evidence to networks and to clients.

Outdoor advertising: In most of the top 100 markets, billboard and bus card advertising (with the necessary production facilities) is readily available. Very often the lesser areas of bench card, delivery truck, traveling electric sign, handbill, and other forms are available, even including the oldtime sandwich-board man. *All* should be explored in the local market for frequency of impact, and used if the situation warrants.

Radio possibilities: In nine out of ten cases, the TV station is associated in the same building with a "sister" radio station. And in eight out of ten cases, management practice permits the use of one station to promote the other.

In this case the TV promotion manager has available a type of on-the-air promotion that is limited only by his own imagination. He can dub the voices from TV promo trailers, add music, sound effects, a narrator, and produce taped or disc spots with great impact, to be used for radio-only effect.

And in many markets he can buy time on small daytime radio stations in his TV coverage area, and place these spots for promotion of nighttime TV viewing!

And then there's that nutty OTHER! With a firm base of audience promotion designed to inform the mass audience of *what's coming*—on-the-air promotion, newspaper advertising, fan magazine, suburban papers, billboards, direct mail movie flyers, etc.—there remains the almost indefinable area of special promotions—that is, one-shot stunts, wild devices, press agent's dreams of *bits* that attract the mass audience to a *thing*.

How and what are these things? For the most part, the *thing* inspires the *bit* . . . A new series of *Chiller* science-fiction movies prompts a contest, seeking the person with the most terrifying scream . . . The introduction of a new series of movie titles induces a like series of scrambled titles—WHIM DONG ERON ESH is *She Done Him Wrong*—"*And,* if you identify the two stars you receive a transistor radio as well as a five-pound package of . . ."

The very best audience contests—in that they demand continued viewing by the audience—are frowned upon by a number of trade and FCC authorities. Nevertheless, they gain great attention when you offer a foreign sports car as the grand prize for counting the number of times in one week that Station WXXX says: "World's Greatest Boysenberry Exporting Center."

Bathing beauties riding high on convertibles, local bar associations endorsing programs, bowling shows tied in with the efforts of local keglers, water safety documentaries associated with the local Red Cross—any and all special promotions are fair game, *as long as* they have a specific purpose of promoting *more* viewing of a *specific program!*

At the risk of seeming tiresome, this is one point I will make several times: *all* audience promotion, be it a chaste pronouncement in a symphony concert program or the zaniest of treasure hunts in a public park, must be weighed by one simple standard —*is it effective in bringing more viewers to your channel?*

There is in all promotion work a large amount of waste effort —the proverbial "spinning of wheels"—with all principals in the stunt a little happy and nothing accomplished. A curmudgeon of a vice president used to bring some of my lesser promotion dreams back to earth with this little lecture:

"Answer this question, what's your C-and-EPM?" And he would go on: "C-*and*-E—cost-*and*-effort per thousand. Remember this—we all talk about our cost-per-thousand when we sell advertising, be it TV or billboards or skywriting. It's the answer to how much does it cost per thousand viewers or listeners or readers that counts.

"You've got another factor—the amount of time and effort spent by you and your staff, and possibly by other station personnel as well. So when you think about your next promotion stunt, figure first how it weighs out on that C-and-EPM scale!"

Sales Promotion

With the optimistic assumption that everything described above has some positive effect, the next problem is that of *making an effective noise about it*—letting the potential buyer in on what is happening.

The promotion manager must establish and keep open a continuing channel of information to a variety of recipients:

His own general and sales management, and the local sales staff.

The sales representative firm involved in selling his station on a national basis.

Local and national advertising agencies.

Local and national present and potential clients.

At proper times, contacts for sales-oriented periodicals, as *Variety, TV-Radio Daily, Sponsor, Broadcasting, Advertising Age,* etc.

Mechanically, he does this with well-kept-up Addressograph plates; the quality of his sales-oriented mailing pieces is of dubious value if his mailing list is not complete and current. *Creatively,* he achieves attention for his station with well-written and well-documented pieces of information about the virtues of the operation and its management.

But, what if his station's product isn't dominant, doesn't show as Number One in its time period? This, then, is the challenge to the professional skills of the promotion man: *Find* the specialized audience in the rating book, or the implied carry-over from the previous show. Or, best of all, the testimonial letters from the over-weight, overwrought, or overstimulated ladies who persist in writing from out there in television land, and reprint them.

Trade advertising: The forms of sales promotion materials are many and varied but, for reasons of cost alone, the category of trade advertising must be considered as a principal activity.

The promotion man has a number of parties to please when he designs an ad for use in a trade publication—a fact that is readily apparent from even a casual examination of *Broadcasting, Advertising Age, Sponsor* and the rest of the broadcasting trade papers.

One station uses beautiful Washington embassies, replete with "excellencies" and "madames" in native garb, and is content to sign the ads discreetly. Another TV outlet features fat and happy cartoon cows, slogans purloined from one of the earlier editions of the Joe Miller *Joke Book,* and call letters almost as big as the cows. And from the consistency of the advertising, it's quite apparent that *both* managements feel there is value in the effort and justification for the cost!

Certainly a part of the problem of effective trade advertising is in the lack of purpose, or at least wide diversity of purpose, that seems evident. One major market general manager states: "If I had my way, I'd never spend a penny in trade ads. But I send reprints to the sales reps, and it makes 'em happy to think we love 'em enough to spend the money. They sell more for us, so I guess we'll keep it up."

The owner of a smaller market station, and a very big trade advertiser, has a simple goal: "They know my call letters in the big cities, and I can take my pick of good employees when I go out to hire."

One of the country's biggest independents has for years extolled its public service work—church services, traffic safety campaigns, special fund drive programs—in costly full-color trade ads, with the obvious purpose to overcome the stigma of the "indy" as a source of old movies and little else.

The stations of one group ownership lean on hard-selling sales presentations in miniature; another group associates its stations with their communities by featuring business, civic and religious leaders in soft-sell sagas of the "movers and shapers of a dynamic market," asking the reader to draw the inference that these VIPs are at least good friends if not avid fans.

A hard-pressed salesman for one of the trade books, short on his quota for the month, has one almost sure-fire sales technique hidden in his bag of tricks; if wise in his work, he saves it for that near-final extremity. He calls *not* the promotion manager but the general manager, congratulates him on some recent press release, article, or rating triumph, then drops his bombshell: "You know, Joe, it's up to you, but if *I* were in *your* place, I'd have my promotion man do that story up as a letter—over your signature, of course, and maybe with a picture in the corner—you have a recent picture, don't you, Joe? Great way to let the trade know you're still around!"

Whether it be the space salesman's soft-soapery, a provident trade allocation in the promotion budget, or a genuine management urge to take part in continued trade advertising, the promotion manager must be prepared to produce professional materials that will further his management's cause.

But determining that *cause* is rarely easy. His staff colleagues can offer a variety of topics: the chief engineer sees great drama in the difficulties involved in mounting a new transmission facility in a swamp or on the side of a mountain; the program manager is insistent that the newest ratings on his pet show—"Uncle Louie's Playhouse"—have import for the trade; the sales manager visualizes a montage of happy clients standing (with him) in front of their business establishments.

The *why* and *how* of trade advertising and of sales promotion generally become intermingled.

The Broadcasters' Promotion Association made a major effort to get at the roots of sales promotion activity during its 1961 seminar in New York. Leading advertising agency people from top agencies in broadcast advertising—account men and women, media supervisors, time buyers, research directors—took part in panel sessions devoted to trade advertising, direct mail, sales presentation techniques, "gimmick" promotions, and the many other ways that TV stations hope to influence the selection of their own particular offerings for advertising purposes.

The continued and persistent questioning by the BPA membership—350 or so station promotion managers—came down to a pair of basics: 1) do you notice our output? 2) does it influence your thinking, planning, and buying recommendations?

A discreet politician would describe the answers as interesting and varied. It's distinctly unpleasant to hear a candid agency vice president say that his secretary has instructions to throw out any and all direct mail—but important to know that it happens.

Conversely, the statement by a media supervisor that she keeps on file all pertinent station information—maps, program information sheets, trade ad reprints, etc.—and reviews these when making buying recommendations, is bound to make the pulse gallop a trifle.

Multiplied ten times over, the conclusions could only be described by that same politico as inconclusive. The conventioneers consoled themselves with the thought that direct mail specialists are delighted with responses that reach five percent, and we certainly came off better than that!

All of which is a long way around to saying that, as this section began, the promotion manager has a challenge in making an *effective noise* about his station.

In trade advertising, he represents his station in its most favorable light for *what it is:* if hobnobbing with Middle East potentates is its forte, then this is the correct approach; if pre-selling dairy farmers is the station's expertise, the comic milch cows with out-size udders may well be the best possible way of putting one's forefoot forward.

Whatever the promotion manager does in trade advertising, he lets everybody know about it, most specifically with reprints of the ads—with a note from the general manager attached—to all parties even remotely connected with selling, buying, or thinking about his station's wares.

He keeps the mail room machines warm with a variety of other mailings as well: updated coverage area maps, including all basic market information; fact sheets on all commercial programs; reprints of press articles; news items of station activity of all sorts; and anything else that he can find time to produce. And in the producing, he remembers that while there is one secretary in New York assigned to throw everything he writes in the wastebasket, there is another female who is putting it all in a file marked with his call letters!

MERCHANDISING

A somewhat nebulous term, not so clearly definable as the audience and sales promotion categories, *merchandising* has become an inevitable part of the promotion manager's routine of activities. Only in the very largest stations and groups is there a separate man or department with the responsibility; more typically, one person in the promotion office has the duty of being "our merchandising expert."

What does *he* do, or better yet, what is *it?* In a most general definition, broadcast merchandising is the function of aiding the client in selling his product. The *how* is best demonstrated by example:

A client buys a large schedule of announcements on Station X, to introduce a new product to be sold through the two largest types of retail outlets—food and drug stores.

> a.) The client wants the supermarket and drug chain buyers and top executives made aware of this upcoming advertising, to be sure that they will buy his product and have adequate stocks in their warehouses. . . . The station sends samples of the product, with an orchid or a small cake or a pair of theater tickets attached, to the wives of the buyers and executives.

b.) The client wants the retail store managers informed of the advertising schedule, so that they will give his product the best possible shelf and display space. . . . The station sends night letters to a list of store managers, citing the "gigantic advertising campaign that will bring thousands of pre-sold customers to your counters . . ."

c.) The client wants a little bonus exposure on the air, by having his product demonstrated on the station's daytime women's show or in the business news program. . . . This the station often does.

With a hundred variations, this is the basic pattern of the merchandising function. NBC's Max Buck, a pioneer in broadcast merchandising patterns, once wrote a think piece titled "Merchandising or Moochingdising?" citing abuses in the unreasonable demands of clients for what amount to kickbacks on their advertising contract. When a client sends a thousand of his own pre-addressed mailing pieces to you in cartons, with instructions to mail them first class through your own mailing facilities, he is in truth demanding a rebate of the cost of the mailing and the handling as *your* cost for doing business with him.

But, when a client has need for legitimate aid in getting his story and his effort across, it *is* a definite function of the promotion man to come up with prompt and adequate activities that will accomplish this purpose.

Most national agencies demand some form of merchandising action for their clients as a matter of course; some employ field men to call on stations and expedite that action. Equally routine, most stations publish a monthly or quarterly "Merchandiser" containing news of current advertising activity on the station. The mailing pieces are, of course, sent to the proper categories as contained in those up-to-date Addressograph files.

In the early 50's, when TV threatened the commercial existence of radio, it was the radio stations and groups that developed the in-store merchandising plans labeled "Chain Lightning," "Shopper Stopper," "The Market Basket," and many more. The food chains made available preferred display space in their outlets, in return for free spot announcement schedules on the station offering the plan. This then put the radio salesman in the position of selling top retail display space for the client, *if* he bought a suitable (meaning X-hundred dollars a week) schedule on the station represented.

Enforcement of the agreements, mostly through the leg work known as "store checking," made the whole thing a costly business for TV and radio stations. The general spread of the activity among competitors, followed by legal pressures on manufacturers through the Robinson-Patman Act, has greatly reduced this form of merchandising—even to the point that some clients and agencies spell out the fact that they do *not* want any form of this activity done for them!

PUBLICITY

The stereotype of the fast-talking, hat-on-the-back-of-the-head press agent, working to gain as much space as possible for Linda Lovely, star of stage and screen, is—fortunately—worn pretty thin. Publicity might better be termed *press relations* in its support of the TV station. Its function as another part of the over-all promotion scheme is to gain space and attention for the station's programs, talent, special activities—and in the case of the trade press, for station management as well.

But the methods of publicity are much less glamorous than generally thought: press releases, biographies, feature stories, photos, advance program information bulletins and humor items are the staples; and the U.S. mails and the telephone are the principal vehicles.

For the network affiliates, the major share of this press information work is carried out by the networks themselves, with large staffs producing an outpouring of special feature and routine program information to newspapers and fan magazines in all of their markets.

For the larger markets, the nets have "column editors" to provide the name columnists with stories and pictures exclusive to their area.

The advertising agencies of the major network clients frequently compound the mail and telegram barrage with special materials on behalf of their shows, and a few of the independent program producers join in as well.

In short, the newspaper columnists, Sunday and feature editors and listings clerks receive a great deal *more* press information than they can handle—*before* the local station promotion-publicity man gets in the act!

Obviously, this restricts the station's publicity effort for the most part to the areas of local programming—the kiddy show, movie host, sports, news and weather talent, and the special programs and events offered by the station.

But the public does indeed have an interest in local entertainers as well as the stars of network offerings, and the station can achieve a reasonable and continued degree of attention in the local press *if* it has the materials and machinery for the job. And one of the best ways to develop the materials and machinery is to determine from the press people themselves their needs and wants!

Very basically, the matter of deadlines is all-important: the Sunday editor (who probably has a copy desk assignment as well) closes his pages on Thursday, and is most receptive early in the week; the suburban weekly, with its press run on Wednesday night, is best contacted *last* Friday, and the *TV Guide* schedule editor needs accurate information and changes 10 or 12 or even 15 days before the issue is set for the stands. Also, the picture of the kiddy performer in his Santa Claus suit will get an assured cover position if it's ready in October, and the inevitable clown with the giant firecracker gag shot should be presented in April at the latest.

All of this is elementary, but is emphasized here for the simple reason that the last-minute and often frantic nature of TV operation tends to lead its practitioners into "stop-the-presses" thinking. And they won't stop for us!

With *when* they need it established, *what* they need is the second step:

> *Accuracy* in program schedule information is axiomatic.
>
> *Interest—human* interest—in the background, schooling, hobbies, family life of local personalities, has reader appeal.
>
> *What's new*—new programs, new talent, projects for the future, new technical equipment—these items give the columnist the opportunity to let his readers (and his editor) know that he is *informed.*
>
> *Humor*—particularly fluffs on the air—is an almost sure-fire column item with any editor, and to be invented or stolen if nothing

presents itself. Such chestnuts as, "Alex Dreier says that a husband is much like a cigar—not much good after you've let it go out," have run the gamut from the *Chicago Tribune* to the Open Switch Gazette.

And there's much more—as varied as the interests of the local columnists.

But so far we've examined the needs of the largely local, consumer press. Publicity in the *trade magazines* is another area of press relations important to the local station—if it is important to have trade advertising, then it is equally important to have representation on the editorial pages of these same publications.

What are they most likely to use? Promotions and job changes *always;* deaths, marriages, births, in that order and *usually.*

Beyond these generalities, certain of the weeklies and monthlies demonstrate major areas in which they are most receptive. *Variety,* everyman's bible of "show biz," has a strong broadcast section, and within it is strongly oriented to the programming side of the industry. Program policies, buys of film packages and syndicated shows, even reviews of local shows, are well received.

On the other hand, *Sponsor* has its greatest interest in who buys television time, and why; in client and agency action.

And *Broadcasting,* everyman's bible of broadcasting, shows its forte in reporting the action of broadcast management, in the erection of new antennas and the purchase of fleets of mobile equipment.

Bi-weekly *Television Age* and monthly *Television* scale themselves to the levels of network activity for the most part, while *Billboard* has its metier in the pop music radio stations, and *Advertising Age* acknowledges broadcasting as a part of the over-all national advertising function.

As with local press contacts, determining *whom* and *when* to contact is axiomatic in trade press publicity. Some use pictures—of those new towers, mobile units or color studios; others feature shots of contract signings and girls in bathing suits. Personal checking will indicate this, including the obvious fact that *Variety* doesn't use *any.*

Publicity, then, as with the other areas of station promotion, demands: 1) realistic, organized procedures; and 2) creative imagination. For the local station, it is imperative that the publicity effort be closely coordinated with all of the other areas of audience promotion, sales promotion and merchandising activity—in a very real sense functioning as a news service *reporting on* these segments of the whole.

A final and personal comment on publicity: In many years of work in this area, I have been burned only once in following a policy of being completely honest with members of the press—and I consider this a very good percentage.

Responsible writers, columnists and editors have a "Front Page" tradition to dig for their story, good or bad; so do our responsible electronic journalists. To withhold the true story of something your management doesn't want put before the public is dangerous on many counts; to bare the facts and request that a confidence be kept is an act of mutual professional stature.

There is but one somber and thought-provoking aspect to this: the station management must first of all be honest with its own promotion or press relations man!

EXPLOITATION

If being in charge of advertising makes one an advertiser, and the promotion function connotes a promoter, then the head of exploitation work must absorb the onus of *exploiter*—a sinister label that at the very least conjures up a vision of the nocturnal seizure of blondes for shipment to the Casbah and that fate worse than death.

The term came into use at NBC New York in the early 1950's, when a venerable movie press agent named Al Rylander was given a small corner in the net's publicity section, a smaller-yet budget, a couple of large assistants—and a free hand to cut across the departmentalized channels of audience promotion, publicity, and programming.

The results were dramatic, sometimes astonishing, and always antic—the "exploitation suggestion kits" sent to the affiliated stations from the Siberia of NBC Press became collectors' items . . .

"Send a man out in a Jimmie Durante mask. To the first ten people who say 'Hey, ain't you supposed to be Jimmie Durante,' or something like that, give them a *gift*—a TV set, or a couple of tickets to a TV show, or *anything."* Because of that small budget, the idea men of Siberia couldn't provide the Durante masks, let alone the gifts. But they did offer the address of a source!

Another: "Fasten a bathtub to the top of a station wagon, and have a girl in the tub in a strapless bathing suit (this was before "bikini" became part of the language). Drive around downtown areas slowly, and when friendly people call to ask the girl why she is in the tub, she answers; 'I'm taking my bath early, so I'll be ready to watch Sid Caesar and Imogene Coca at nine tonight on Channel 5!' "

A standard suggestion for the handling of visits by NBC network celebrities, and a never-ending source of humor for the promotion managers who received the telegrams, began: "Have your mayor and the town's high school band at the gates of the city . . ."

Exploitation has come to greener pastures (Al Rylander became a veepee of NBC!) and acquired a promotion-integrated patina of sophistication, but the lesson of occasional zany, all-out, pure audience promotion corn must never be forgotten.

SUMMARY

And on the incongruous note of "corn" the whole area of advertising-promotion-publicity may be summed up. For if "corn" is the gang at the piano bar singing "Heart of My Heart" as opposed to the fans of woodwind quintettes, the subscribers to *Reader's Digest* versus *Saturday Review,* or the homeowners who put pink ceramic flamingos in their front lawns contrasted to the renters of penthouses, then the promotion man is up to his elbows in corn in his every activity.

The promotion manager and (hopefully) his assistants must wear many hats: the typical day is a jumble of sales managers demanding mailings for their clients, kiddy entertainers complaining that "Commander Fuzz" on the other channel gets more publicity, peddlers of advertising space on the walls of laundromats, and possibly a station manager who needs a quick 20-minute script for the speech he's giving *today* at the Kiwanis meeting.

In his fireman's helmet, leaping from one brush blaze to another, the promotion man all too often runs out of time and energy before the concept, let alone the execution, of the truly *big* campaign or stunt ever evolves.

But he *must* find this time and energy, and most probably does in solitary contemplation during the small hours of the evening and morning, for such is the nature of the business. And, other than a capacity for sustaining the impact of many people and little sleep, what capabilities should the promotion man possess?

A reasonable technical knowledge of printing, from reprints of press clippings to billboard paper and everything in-between.

A similar knowledge of television production—slides, films, videotapes, and the rest.

Sound administrative skills, including the control of a budget only slightly below programming and engineering.

An ability to indulge in verbal communication with clients, actors, printers, columnists, managers, home office brass.

A capacity for food and drink that enables him to carry a reasonable load in one package.

Above all, a sound writing and editing skill that puts forth his management's best foot in a crisp, literate and professional style. (As an afterthought, it doesn't hurt if he can play a chorus of "Heart of My Heart" on the piano for that gang down at the corner!)

PART FOUR

SALES MANAGEMENT FOR THE TELEVISION STATION

CHAPTER 12

The Business
of Research

BY JULIUS BARNATHAN

ABC Television Network, New York

Now Vice President and General Manager of the ABC Television Network, Mr. Barnathan has had a wide background in research that began at Kenyon & Eckhardt, Inc., New York advertising agency. He joined the American Broadcasting Company in 1954 as a supervisor of ratings, subsequently becoming Manager of Research and then Director of Research. Other important management assignments followed, leading to his present position. Mr. Barnathan holds a Bachelor's degree in mathematics and statistics from Brooklyn College where he was Phi Beta Kappa, and a Master's degree in mathematical statistics from Columbia University. His professional associations include the American Statistical Association and the Radio-TV Research Council, of which he has been President. He is currently on the Board of the Broadcast Rating Council.

M ANY station managers think of research as being synonymous with ratings or audience measurements. Actually, however, research encompasses much more. It means finding out about a station's audience: characteristics (where they live, what they do, how much they earn, what they own); audience measurements (do they watch your station, at what times, for how long?); or qualitative data (do they like your station, do they think well of your personalities, news department, management?). Research also involves special studies to determine the effectiveness of TV advertising.

MARKET DATA

Market characteristics data are available from the decennial census and from several trade sources such as Survey of Buying Power, *Sales Management,* Standard Rate and Data Service, and R. L. Polk Co. In addition, the local Chamber of Commerce, tax bureaus, and state authorities have comprehensive information that can be used to define the characteristics of a market. Utilization of this information in ads, booklets, meetings, etc. helps to bring to the attention of time buyers and advertisers the dynamics of your market. It must be remembered that before a buyer determines which station he will use, he must be sold on the market. Furthermore, the market is competing with other markets for its share of the TV dollar and thus it is the station's responsibility to see to it that the market's share of the dollar is healthy and growing. If the respective market is not getting its share of television expenditure, then this area of research should be emphasized. Where possible, a joint effort among all stations in the market is worthwhile for the purpose of familiarizing all potential advertisers with the desirability of advertising in that community. Too often stations within a market are so competitive that they neglect the fact that they have something important in common—the same market to sell. Every station manager should have a set of market facts about its entire area. These facts should be in a form that can easily be used in sales brochures and other sales devices.

RATING DATA

For selling his own advertising time, the station manager's most important research material is rating data or audience measurements. Ratings in the past several years have come under serious attack by the government, critics, intellectuals and by many industry people. While certain irregularities were pointed out at Congressional hearings, it is interesting to note that there was no evidence of "rigging" or "fixing" of ratings by any broadcaster. What was disclosed was many of the operational flaws in the *techniques* used by each rating service. Some of these flaws were known to the sophisticated researcher but unknown to the layman. Subsequently, the television industry has formed the Broadcast Rating Council to audit rating services and to set minimum standards.

Ratings are the means by which broadcasters measure their "gate" or box office. The principle involved is that of sampling. Inasmuch as it is impossible to know exactly what every person is watching at any moment, a sampling of viewing activity is used to estimate how many persons are viewing television and what they are watching. Indeed, this principle of sampling is used today in almost every facet of American life. When a jury is picked, it is supposed to represent the entire public; when a doctor takes a drop of blood from a person's finger, he is sampling; manufacturers test products on their assembly line.

Sampling of people must follow the same basic principles, which are:

1) Define that which is to be sampled, such as television homes in a specific coverage area, women in a certain age group, etc.

2) Try to select a probability sample so representative of the whole that the selection of any element is also representative. If the cost is too high, a modified design should be used.

3) Try to get optimum cooperation from the sample homes. This will minimize any bias (error) that might occur due to non-response.

4) Be sure of proper supervision of the field staff and the tabulating staff. This will assure accurate reporting of the data.

The above principles are basic to any good sample survey. In television, the rating data, despite their many flaws, tend to state with a reasonable degree of accuracy the size of the audience of most programs. If ratings are used as *estimates* and not as hard-fact yardsticks, they can be excellent tools.

AUDIENCE MEASUREMENTS

Actually, the very term, rating, is a misnomer in this situation. Usually, a rating is a subjective evaluation of something, such as a motion picture. However, as a generic term, ratings in television mean audience measurements—how many homes or people are viewing a program, or programs, or station, or whatever. Thus, audience measurements are *quantitative* measures or estimates of the number of homes reached. Within this generic area of "ratings" there are three basic measuring terms: rating, sets-in-use, and share of audience.

Rating is the percentage of all homes (or individuals) in a population that represents the potential audience of a given broadcast.

$$\text{Rating} = \frac{\text{No. of TV homes watching a program}}{\text{No. of TV homes in the population}}$$

Sets-in-use is the percentage of all homes with one or more receivers in use during a moment or any interval of time.

$$\text{Sets-in-Use} = \frac{\text{No. of TV homes tuned in to television}}{\text{No. of TV homes in the population}}$$

Share of audience is the relationship between the sets tuned in to a specific program as compared with the total number of sets tuned to any television in a specific area.

$$\text{Share of Audience} = \frac{\text{No. of TV homes watching a program}}{\text{No. of TV homes tuned on}}$$

Now if we divide the numerator and denominator by the number of TV homes in the population:

$$\text{Share of Audience} = \frac{\dfrac{\text{No. of TV homes watching a program}}{\text{No. of TV homes in population}}}{\dfrac{\text{No. of TV homes tuned on}}{\text{No. of TV homes in population}}}$$

we get

$$\text{Share of Audience} = \frac{\text{Rating}}{\text{Sets-in-Use}}$$

or

$$\text{Ratings} = \text{Share of Audience} \times \text{Sets-in-Use.}$$

or

$$\text{Sets-in-Use} = \frac{\text{Rating}}{\text{Share of Audience}}$$

Thus we find that these three measures have a distinct relationship with each other.

Ratings and sets-in-use are absolute measures (they always have the same denominator or base). Therefore, ratings or sets-in-use can be averaged by simply adding up the total and dividing by the number of periods being averaged. For example:

	Rating
Mon. 8:00 PM	18
8:30 PM	24
9:00 PM	30
Average	72 ÷ 3 = 24

Share of audience cannot be averaged directly. For example:

	Rating	Share	Sets-in-Use
7:15 PM	3	10	30
8:30 PM	42	70	60
Average	22.5	50	45

A 40% share of audience would be incorrect. The correct share is 50%. In other words, total rating points divided by total sets-in-use points equals the average share of audience. Let us look at the basic relationship again:

Ratings = Share of Audience x Sets-in-Use.

Just from this relationship, it is evident that:

The rating attained by a program is dependent upon the sets in use. The more television sets tuned on during a particular time period, the higher is the potential audience or rating. The share of audience is a better measure for comparison of two programs in two different time periods since it eliminates the effect of sets-in-use.

Now that we have defined the three fundamental measures, let's take note of several other terms that are used extensively:

Viewers-per-set is the average number of viewers per TV home tuned to a program, or:

$$\text{Viewers-per-set} = \frac{\text{Total TV Viewers}}{\text{Total TV Homes Tuned}}$$

Station coverage area is the land area containing a station's audience.

Cumulative rating ("cume") is the percentage of *different* TV homes viewing two or more programs.

Finally, it must be remembered that the rating performance of any program is relative to: 1) the type of program it is; 2) the time period it is in; 3) the competition it faces; 4) its lead-in programming, and 5) the over-all strength of the station. Thus, more than one factor helps determine the audience size of a particular program, and all factors should be considered in analyzing a program's success or failure.

THE RATING SERVICES

There are several rating services, each using a different method of measuring audiences. This is one of the main reasons why at times they will come up with different results. Factors contributing to this disparity are: 1) techniques differ; 2) rating periods will vary; 3) the survey area differs. When some of these factors have been eliminated, one will find that the ratings from the different services generally are in fairly close agreement.

The two leading local rating services are: Nielsen Station Index (NSI), and American Research Bureau (ARB). Both organizations use diaries to record viewing data. NSI supplements the diaries with audimeters and recordimeters, electronic devices attached to the TV sets to measure TV tuning activity.

Another technique generally used to measure TV viewing is the "telephone coincidental," the conducting of telephone interviews throughout the duration of a given program or tuning period.

This method is employed by Hooper, Trendex and ARB. Still another widely used method is the "personal roster recall," in which respondents are shown a list of programs and stations and are asked to indicate which they were exposed to during the measured time span. This method is used by Pulse.

The final product of all rating services is the syndicated report on the television viewing in the market which is sold to stations, agencies and advertisers. Data presented include:

Metro Rating Data—ratings, shares, and sets-in-use information pertaining to the respective metropolitan area where the local stations get about 98% of their total viewing. This information is reported for each quarter hour of the period of the survey.

Total Homes Reached—an estimate of the number of total homes reached by the station in the entire coverage area in each quarter hour.

Audience Composition Data—estimates of total viewers, and their breakdown by men, women, teens (12-18) and children.

The rating books generally show ratings by quarter hour, but some services show averages for the Monday through Friday daytime ratings so as to eliminate the larger fluctuations possible in these time periods of lower ratings. In addition, statistical summaries by day, for each station, are available in the books. Some services provide additional information, such as data that isolates young viewers (18-35). Of course, all kinds of special tabulations or studies that further refine the basic data can be ordered from the rating services. These analyses can provide vital programming and sales information.

APPLYING RESEARCH TO PROGRAMMING

Having taken this brief review of terminology, let us proceed to consider the application of research. Much of the criticism of ratings have been concerned with abuses of their use. Ratings are not the be-all and end-all of what programs should go on the air; rather, they must be used with discretion and with understanding.

One of the primary uses of ratings is as a guide for programming decisions. If the audience characteristics of a particular program are known, it can be "slotted" where it can get maximum audience and then can be sold to an advertiser interested in reaching that type of audience. Knowing the type of audience a program reaches also enables a manager to program his station in a smooth and orderly fashion so as to achieve "flow of audience"— that is, viewers staying tuned from one program to the following program, and so on. This flow, especially in prime time, is vital to success.

Public service programs, for example, often interrupt audience flow. If an entertainment program is very strong, the scheduling of a public service show in front of it may not cut down its audience drastically. On the other hand, if a public service show precedes a weak show that depends on and feeds off its lead-in, the effect can be disastrous. This can be illustrated in the case of *The Flintstones* and *Dickens and Fenster,* which were scheduled back-to-back. When a public service show was scheduled in front of *The Flintstones,* it did not materially reduce the latter's audience. But when *The Flintstones* was pre-empted for a public service show, *Dickens and Fenster,* which followed it, did very poorly. Thus, it may be seen that an understanding of the audience characteristics enables a station manager and a program manager to maximize a program's potential audience and to encourage audience flow from one program to another.

USING RATINGS TO SELL TIME

The other major use of ratings is in selling the time of a station. Most stations set the prices of their commercial availabilities according to the ratings the station has enjoyed in the various time periods. National advertisers greatly depend on these ratings to determine their purchases in a market, using as their evaluative measure, "cost per thousand" (CPM) homes. This is best defined as:

$$\text{Cost Per Thousand Homes (CPM)} = \frac{\text{Cost}}{\text{No. of TV homes reached (in 000's)}}$$

Other measures that are used are CPM Viewers, CPM Men, CPM Women, and CPM Children. Each of these is derived in the same way. While these are good measures of efficiency, they should not be the only criteria for buying. There are too many other factors that are important. Some of these are:

Cumulative Reach: The number of different homes reached is important. A rating that reveals total home impressions does not indicate the extent to which the total represents different homes, or whether it represents a hard core of viewers reached repetitively. The cumulative reach as well as the total rating should be known.

Audience Composition: An advertiser may be selling to men or women or children. The audience composition of the programs must be known so that he can be guided accordingly.

Audience Characteristics: The advertiser will be interested in the kind of audience reached (e.g., young or old people, large families, small families, upper or lower income).

Program Type: A commercial done live in a personality show frequently has more impact than filmed commercials in a film show. News programs have sponsorship values far beyond the ratings of the program; the same is true for public service specials.

Merchandisability: Many advertisers want to merchandise their television schedule to their salesmen, buyers and customers.

Program Environment: A commercial may have more impact within a program than at a station break. The number of commercials in and around any other advertiser's commercial may affect audience reaction.

As can be seen, there are many more things to watch than merely cost-per-thousand.

SPECIAL STUDIES

Besides utilizing syndicated services, a good station manager should always know his public's attitudes toward his programming, news and public service efforts. This can only be done by periodic, special surveys designed specifically for the market. These can help a manager know how well his station is regarded and if he is fulfilling his public responsibility. Too often a station manager believes he is talking to his public when he meets with the local government officials, educators, clergy and social scientists. This is not enough. These groups often represent their own point of view, one that may differ from the public's attitudes.

Other kinds of surveys can have direct commercial values. TV effectiveness studies and impact studies can be extremely helpful in keeping advertisers sold on TV.

SUMMARY

Research, as we have seen, involves many areas. It is the manager's job to know his market, his public and his station through the relevant research that provides these data. Such detailed information will help him promote the advantages of his market so that national advertisers will spend their money there. The research data will also help him convince the advertisers that do use his market to specifically use his station. Finally, research will help him select entertainment and public service programs and so schedule them that the station will receive maximum viewing.

If a television station is located in one of the top 75 markets, it should be able to afford a small research staff (director, one assistant, one clerk and two secretaries). Station managers will find that the proper use of research material will contribute to revenues sums well in excess of the department's cost. There is no question that research is a valuable tool enabling a station manager to obtain his objectives.

CHAPTER 13

Sales Management for the Network Affiliate

BY *ALBERT JOHN GILLEN*

WPRO-TV, Providence, Rhode Island

A native of New York City, Mr. Gillen was graduated magna cum laude from Syracuse University. His professional background includes television and radio sales, as well as advertising agency experience. He is now General Sales Manager of WPRO-TV in Providence, Rhode Island, owned by Capital Cities Broadcasting Corporation.

A NYONE in television—be he general manager, program manager, promotion manager, especially sales manager—must be convinced that television is: 1) the most effective form of mass communication yet devised by man, and 2) as such, entertains, informs, educates and makes profits. All of these attributes make the television business one of great satisfaction, great responsibility and as American as the backyard cook-out. Since it is also basically American to believe in the profit motive it is elementary, but nevertheless important, to realize that there is no conflict between serving the public interest and making a profit. It is the job of the sales manager to assure that there is an adequate income base produced for the television station.

Inasmuch as every station is granted a license by the Federal Communications Commission to operate for a three-year period, it is part of the sales manager's responsibility to conduct the station's business with discretion and integrity to assure the preservation and subsequent renewal of the station's license. Since the majority of stations are—and, if not, should be—members of the NAB (National Association of Broadcasters) and, as such, subscribe to the NAB Code, sales management within the Code rules is essential. The Code outlines, in specific detail, guidelines as agreed upon by broadcasters themselves covering: 1) length of commercials, 2) number of commercials within specific time periods, and 3) suggested commercial limitations within programs and on break positions between programs. As it is the responsibility and privilege of the board of directors, general manager and/or owners to outline the desired company policy and objectives, it is also clearly the responsibility of the sales manager to operate within the framework of those policies. Perhaps this can best be restated as the need for him to communicate, cooperate, and work under general management and over the personnel reporting to him.

INTER-RELATION WITH OTHER DEPARTMENTS

The sales manager and the Sales Department inter-relate with all other departments and department heads within the operation of a television station. (See table of organization chart, page 56—Ed.) Since so many other departments are affected by the conduct of the Sales Department, one cannot over-emphasize the importance of efficient and effective cooperation.

Program Department: It is extremely important to keep the program manager informed as to the needs of the buyers of television advertising. With much of today's concentration on early and late fringe-minute announcements, the Program Department with this knowledge can schedule programming to deliver the maximum inventory of these announcements. In many cases the local advertiser is interested in sponsoring programs and program segments such as "News" and "Weather" shows, and this information is important to pass along to the Program Department. As an example, children personality shows have been an effective source of income for many stations in recent years. By ascertaining the current and future trends of advertisers' requirements both locally and nationally, the sales manager can provide the Program Department with the information for programming to meet the immediate and future needs for sales inventory.

Within the Program Department, the production manager has the responsibility of producing local commercials either for clients themselves or in cooperation with local advertising agencies. To a large extent, the effectiveness of a local advertising campaign will be due to the quality of the commercial itself, whether this be video tape, film or live. The ability and technical skills of the production manager—as well as of the Continuity Department under the production manager—are of major importance to the sales manager. If the Sales Department creates an effective buy for a local account and the Production Department produces an ineffective commercial, it is virtually impossible to produce results for the account. That particular account then becomes a short-term buyer instead of a long-term customer.

Traffic Department: In many stations the Traffic Department is directly responsible to the program manager. Specific details of every account scheduled must be quickly transmitted by the Sales Department to the Traffic Department in order to insure correct handling of on-the-air schedules. Typically, this information will include film or video tape numbers and rotation of various commercials within an advertiser's schedule. If they are live commercials, they also will include the video shots and audio copy.

The merging of many companies in recent years has greatly increased the number of multiple advertisers. Product lines have been expanded. It is not unusual to find a particular television advertiser purchasing a 12-spot-a-week schedule within which will be carried as many as 12 different commercials for five or six different products within a month. Proper handling of such intricate scheduling is of the utmost importance. (See Chapter 16—Ed.)

Promotion Department: Promotional efforts of the station on many occasions can contribute to the successful completion of a sale, when a promotion manager is informed as to advertisers' needs. Many stations direct a large part of their Promotion Department efforts toward establishing and building on-the-air personalities who become available for personal appearances in shopping centers, retail stores and theaters. This can develop into an important source of revenue when such appearances are coordinated with advertising campaigns at these various places of business. The result is a successful promotion for the television station, the production of revenue to the station and the achievement of sales results for the advertisers involved.

Business Department: Important sources of vital information to the sales manager can be obtained from the business manager, such as: credit information; analysis of "sell-out" position of inventory; account analysis—that is, comparative figures of volume of business done by accounts and account categories in current months compared to previous months; analysis of income by months for budgeting and forecasting.

REVENUE

There are three sources of advertising revenue for stations with network affiliations: network (20-25%); national and regional spot (50-60%); and local (20-25%).

Network: The network produces or purchases programs for subsequent sale to national advertisers to be televised on their owned stations and independently-owned affiliates. The compensation received by these independent stations for carrying such network commercial programs is based on two factors: 1) the network hourly base rate of the particular affiliate (usually based on the audience the affiliate reaches); 2) the percentage of this base rate which the network pays to the affiliate (usually approximately 30%, but which may vary depending upon negotiations between the network and the affiliate).

National and Regional Spot: Bought by a national or regional advertiser who wishes to achieve a specific marketing objective by "spotting" his television advertising in certain specific markets, this is the most important source of revenue to the typical network affiliate. To produce this revenue for the station, a national representative firm maintaining offices in the important advertising centers in the country is hired on a commission percentage basis, or a group of mutually-owned stations may form its own "rep" company. (See Chapter 15 for a detailed discussion—Ed.)

Local: This category of revenue consists of a wide and varied number of local companies purchasing time from the station either directly or through local advertising agencies.

SALES DEPARTMENT ORGANIZATIONAL STRUCTURE

The typical sales department of a television station will look something like this:

Local Sales Manager: Administers and directs the local

sales force, usually comprising four to six men. He reports to general sales manager.

Sales Service Traffic Department: Responsible for maintenance of inventory logs. Produces availability sheets and transmits of sales information to Program Traffic.

National Sales Coordinator: Maintains contact with local branch offices of national accounts. Services food brokers.

Sales Promotion Manager: Produces printed sales tools for local and national sales force. Compiles research analysis of station, administers merchandising services offered by station to advertisers.

SALES ANALYSIS

It is not enough merely to sell. There must be an understanding of the significance and implications of one's activities. Toward this end, sales analysis is important to form judgments regarding: budgeting; projecting; evaluation of performance; pricing; inventory control.

Budgeting: Used intelligently, budgets are one of the most important tools a sales manager has. He must run the budget, however, and not allow the budget to run him. The cliché, "Yes! But look how I stayed *within* the budget," may be the last statement uttered as the ship slowly fills and sinks into the emerald sea. Budgeting does not necessarily mean only the control of expenses. The proper use of budgeting includes sales goals and expense goals.

Budgeting for sales goals can be done by 13-week periods throughout the year, or by calendar months, fiscal months, or even a breakdown by weeks. These budget figures should include separately the various categories of sales revenue, such as: network, national and regional spot, and local. In budgeting for expense goals, include categories such as: salaries; commissions; sales promotion; travel and entertainment; supplies; and that best of all possible categories, "miscellaneous." Budgeting in this manner will then provide the *profit goal* for the Sales Department and the ingredients for the manager or owner of the station to project over-all profit objectives.

After the budgets are formulated, according to the needs of the station the budgets themselves can be adjusted as matters of expediency or change dictate. Similarly, the projection can be adjusted. It is perhaps advisable to retain budget figures and change projections so that at the end of any fiscal or calendar year, the unchanged budget figures can be used as an appraisal and measure of how well the original budgets were prepared.

Projecting: Projections can be made for the three major categories of revenue by breaking down the station's share of market in numerous categories, as follows.

Explanation Column	*Network*	*National*	*Local*
Share of dollars *in* the market can be obtained through monitors of competing stations or (in the event of a three-station market) from published FCC figures.	....% $.....	....% $.....	....% $.....
Share of dollars compared to other comparable markets can be obtained from comparisons made by NAB or TV Bureau of Advertising.	....% $.....	....% $.....	....% $.....

Total projected figures made up from these comparisons can be broken down on a month-by-month basis by simply figuring the expected percentage revenue per month from the actual percentage breakdowns in previous years. Another tool for projecting is to build up figures by taking the various ingredients of the program schedule and evaluating the potential return from specific programs or time segments in all three revenue categories. This type of analysis may bring to light, for instance, that the potential return for local revenue may be very limited due to the fact that the schedule does not contain enough good local programs to serve the needs of local advertisers. Or, it may indicate that the program schedule is overweighted with too much children's programming and does not have enough inventory in adult audience "minute availabilities."

Monthly figures delineating the percentage of sell-out of various time periods and specific programs will indicate potential revenue for projection purposes and also the current worth of the particular program on the station. For instance, if a particular daytime program, such as a half-hour syndicated show five days a week 10:00-10:30 A.M., has a maximum inventory of 30 one-minute announcements a week and over the course of a six-month period the number of spots sold within the show vary from one to three per week, the highest sell-out percentage the show has ever had is 10%. Although there may be other reasons to retain the program on the schedule (such as station image, community service, etc.), from a *sales* standpoint the program is clearly an inadequate income producer.

Evaluation of Performance: The performance of the Sales Department can be evaluated against many standards: 1) station's share of audience compared to station's share of dollars in the market; 2) station's share of revenue in all categories compared to stations in markets of *like* population or *like* revenue; 3) if station is part of a multiple-station group, comparisons can be made with other stations in the group; 4) total yearly revenue in all categories should be compared to budget estimates and forecast estimates.

In evaluating performance, all factors affecting the station's revenue should be weighed. These might include: 1) change in business economy during the year; 2) increase or decrease in time rates during the year; 3) unusual circumstances, such as: strikes, relocation of tower, addition of new stations in market or new stations in market's fringe area; 4) sharp changes downward or upward in station's audience position.

Pricing: Rate cards are formulated in part by research comparisons available such as ARB or Nielsen. Based on that research material, most national and regional spot advertisers predicate a buy in a market and a choice of a particular station on a CPM basis (cost per thousand viewers reached). This is one of the criteria used in buying and it is, therefore, necessary for a station to use this as one of its guidelines in pricing its announcements and programs for sale. A most important additional ingredient to be used in formulating the rate card of a station is the price that is determined by the customers themselves. There are many factors within this category that may dictate an increase or decrease in the station's pricing. Over and above the cost per thousand basis, one of the factors tending to *decrease* a station's price may be a less than complete coverage by the station of the total metropolitan market it serves due to technical inadequacies such as lower power, or lower tower height than competitors. A station's prices also might be decreased by a plethora of certain types of programming, such as feature films or children's programs. Factors tending to justify substantial *increases* over cost per thousand guidelines may be: outstanding children's personalities; well-established news personalities; exclusive features, such as being the only TV station with feature films in the market; ownership of particularly desirable syndicated programs; outstanding image of the station itself.

Inventory Control: Supply and demand will influence to a large degree the total number of announcements and the type programs the station may have sold. To maximize the return from the station's inventory is perhaps the most critical responsibility of the sales manager. In many instances an immediate sale can be made to an advertiser merely by selling this account the highest rated spots on the station. However, this may not be the best possible schedule with which to produce maximum results for that particular client. By carefully screening the current availabilities, the sales manager often is able to suggest a schedule to this client which may increase the expenditure by a small amount and the potential results to the advertiser by a great amount. Or he may, at no increase in expenditure, suggest changes in a client's original schedule which may improve the results obtained from a client's dollars. Such advice will reflect the sales manager's knowledge of the sales impact of the station's personalities or various programs—impact that may not be revealed in rating books or research analyses. Such prudent control of his inventory may enable a sales manager to utilize his availabilities for the greatest number of advertisers, for best results.

SALES TOOLS

The Sales Promotion Department, in conjunction with the sales manager, is responsible for producing the many and varied sales tools utilized in the day-to-day buying and selling of television time.

Research brochures, outlining the station's NRB (National Research Bureau) and NSI (Neilsen Station Index) rating history as regards total station share and individual program performance, should be provided to the station's representative firm, national and regional advertising agencies, and local sales staff. In the event that new programs are placed on the program schedule at a time when the research organizations are not conducting a survey, special coincidental surveys may be taken to provide immediate information as to audience performance of these new shows. Special coverage studies can be purchased from the major research firms to establish the station's effective coverage area and its circulation in each county within that coverage area. A special analysis for each program on the station's schedule can be made up to indicate the percentage of men, women and children viewing a particular program series. Research trends of a program over a period of years can be an important sales tool to interest advertisers.

Program sheets are another sales aid. They usually include pictures of the personalities, sales success stories of various advertisers using the program in the past, time of show, length of show, research history and cost. Detailed information is usually supplied for feature film programming, such as: movie title, stars, year the picture was released, date and time the station will program these features. In the case of special events programming—such as sporting events, special news shows and documentaries—it is important to provide simple, factual, immediate information to the national representative firm and local salesmen for use in making sales calls. As there can be no research material available for a new program scheduled in the immediate future, the history and background of the particular program *subject* very often comprise the content of this sales piece.

The coverage map is another sales tool. It outlines the area reached by the station, provides information on the make-up of the area's population, food sales, drug sales and other market statistics. This information is particularly effective with the local advertiser who often is unable to reach suburban dwellers with newspaper advertising as effectively and as efficiently as he can reach the same population with TV. The Television Bureau of Advertising and the NAB provide a great deal of factual information for stations to use in preparing material illustrating the impact of the sight-sound-motion demonstration ability of the television medium.

Currently, many local business concerns are managed by businessmen who have grown up during the era of television, and they are apt to be more aware of the impact of TV than are their older counterparts who were more comfortable with, and more oriented to, newspaper advertising. The area of local advertising perhaps holds the key to more dramatic potential increases in station sales revenue than any other category.

PERSONNEL MANAGEMENT

Remuneration: Secretarial, clerical and administrative personnel such as sales promotion, sales service and merchandising employees are usually salaried. But for salesmen there is a tremendous variety of compensation plans, such as: straight salary; salary plus bonus; salary plus commission; straight commission; commission against drawing account; and various combinations of all of these. Regardless of which system is used, a salesman's compensation ideally should be based on the following principles: 1), an established guarantee providing him and his family with a reasonable standard of living to begin with; 2), a commission percentage as a standard base figure (for example, 10%) but depending, of course, on the actual station market; 3), an additional percentage figure (such as, for example, 1%) to be paid on his over-all production if the salesman exceeds the monthly quota assigned to him; 4), frequent participation in competition, so that the salesman can satisfy his own needs for recognition of his achievements—such competitions include sales contests, special sales incentive plans, special awards, and so on.

Sales Lists: Detailed lists of every potential local account in the market should be made up with index cards showing account name, major personnel of the account, brief history of the account, estimated advertising budget, past use of television, and the name of the person responsible for advertising decisions. One set of these index cards can be used as the master sales list for the station management, with duplicate sets provided to the salesmen assigned specific accounts. The administration by the sales manager and/or the local sales manager of these sales lists is most important. Changes should be made as frequently as needed, particularly if accounts on a particular salesman's list are inactive for too long a period of time. Records as to calls made on these accounts, results obtained, and other sales information can be recorded on the back of the card for future reference.

Sales Reports: Simple and easy-to-keep records can provide the salesmen with the basic information on call-backs, or to recall special campaigns an account may have had previously (such as back-to-school sales, white sales, etc.). These can also provide the guideline to the local sales manager for evaluating a salesman's performance as well as a basis for consultation between salesman and local sales manager as to where the salesman may need help in solving a particular problem. It is most important for the local sales manager to work closely enough with the salesmen under him so that he understands their problems, supervises their activities and yet does not interfere with their own individual effectiveness in doing their jobs. While financial remuneration is of extreme importance, a good salesman is motivated by many things other than money. One of the strongest motivating forces of a salesman is his need for achieving weekly and monthly goals of *his own* (such as making a sale, setting a record in the department, bringing in an account for the first time, winning a sales contest, or the like). Obviously, the salesman should be recognized by the department head when he achieves any of such goals.

Local Sales Manager: Familiar with the problems and techniques involved in handling local advertisers, many of whom will look to the station to fill the role of advertising consultant, in many cases the sales manager is sought by local advertising agencies who require more information and assistance than do the larger staffed national agencies. This does not mean that the local agency is inferior to the national agency but that, having smaller staffs than do the major national agencies, the local agencies will more frequently utilize the station's facilities such as production, art, photography and video tape. The administration, follow-up, and directing of the local sales staff is the responsibility of the local sales manager as is the handling of local account assignments, sales reports, local sales quotas, local sales budgeting and forecasting. An able, aggressive local sales manager can stimulate and direct the local sales staff to materially increase a station's net profit. The local sales manager can be compensated in many ways but it is important to provide an adequate base salary plus an incentive in the form of a bonus or over-ride commission percentage to insure maximum performance in his responsibilities.

National Representative Firm: While the Sales Department at the station is under the direct responsibility and control of the general sales manager, relationship with the sales representative firm is somewhat different. A rep firm maintains its own staff in the major buying centers of the country and usually represents any number of stations, often 10 to 30, in non-competitive markets. These firms are paid a commission to secure national and regional spot business for those stations they represent.

The general sales manager travels to the various offices maintained by the rep firm to provide a constant flow of information to the executive personnel and the individual salesmen, so that everyone in the representative organization has an intimate knowledge of just what the station is doing in performance, programming, pricing, etc. Frequent visits to the advertising centers and frequent calls with the rep salesman are the keys to securing the maximum share of national dollars for the station. A well-worn suitcase is usually the sign of a successful sales manager. Frequent consultation with his rep firm on budgeting, forecasting, pricing, promotion, research, and programming all serve to create harmonious relations. Benefitting from such close consultation and cooperation, both station and rep firm should prosper.

SERVICE PROGRAMMING

While it is obvious that the sales manager is responsible for producing the revenue of the station, which in turn provides the base for ownership to produce net profit, it is perhaps not so obvious that the successful sales manager provides the commercial income which enables a station to fulfill its role as the holder of a license granted to broadcast in the interest of the public—through public service, information, news, religious, discussion, educational, documentary, political and civic programs. All these are supported and financed by the advertising expenditures of business concerns, flowing through the Sales Department of the television station.

SUMMARY

Television sales management is the art of stimulating local, regional, and national advertising budgets in a market—and then getting a major share of those budgets. The sales manager achieves these goals through the effective direction of his local salesmen and the men of the national representative firm. He arms his salesmen with information about their product, and directs them with his knowledge of the marketplace. Through all this, his function remains an integral part of television station management. The Programming Department cannot entertain the public nor serve the public unless the bills are paid. It is up to sales management to provide those necessary funds—and the profits too. Because profits, as well as programming, are part of the American way of television.

CHAPTER 14

Sales Management for the Independent

BY CHARLES YOUNG

KTTV, Los Angeles, California

Beginning as a local salesman with KTTV in 1952, Mr. Young was subsequently promoted to National Sales Manager and then to his current position of Vice-President in Charge of National Sales. His previous background includes local television production as well as having operated his own publicity office in Hollywood.

A s will have been noted previously, the role of the independent station within the broad spectrum of television broadcasting is truly unique (see Chapter 4—Ed.). There aren't many of us, and our positions vary greatly from the single independent WGN-TV in the great market of Chicago to KPHO-TV in the fifty-third television market of the United States (Phoenix, Arizona) to the four independents now operating in the highly competitive second television market of Los Angeles.

Although our markets vary widely in size, patterns of distribution, set ownership and even viewing habits, we still have many similarities among ourselves in our sales and operational methods. The similarities, including some very elementary points, are:

1) We are all in business to make a profit.

2) We all operate under a federal license requiring a strong contribution to the public interest of the community we serve.

3) We all face intense competition from the three networks, in the form of either affiliated stations or owned-and-operated sta-

tions. (And when there is more than one independent operating, particularly in such major markets as New York and Los Angeles, the competition is fierce.)

4) Our program supply is limited, and costs are high. Therefore we must, or should, depend on a high degree of local creative program effort.

5) We have an obligation not only to properly serve the public interest of our community but, additionally, to provide the *local or regional merchant or manufacturer* access to the sales power of television. (Generally he cannot afford our higher priced network competitor.)

6) Our basic commodity is the longer commercial (one minute, or more on occasion) for which there is a real need both locally, regionally and nationally.

Some of us—because of our market position, by accident, or through just plain luck—enjoy a greater degree of success in dealing with the above similarities but, regardless, it's never dull or "push-button." How a station performs is to a great extent the direct responsibility of sales management—the eyes and ears of an independent station. It is this department's antennae that seek out the competitive factors at work in the market place and provide management with a careful appraisal of them. It is the responsibility of this department to exercise tender control of the station's rate structure—a bad guess in pricing can mean disaster. In effect, the Sales Department is a hub around which all other operational factors are geared. In the highly critical position of an independent, where one wrong decision may take months for recovery, its importance cannot be overemphasized.

A sales manager therefore should possess knowledge of: advertising policies, objectives and personnel of customers and potential customers; broadcasting operations, theory and practice; marketing and sales including basic forecasting, organization, incentives, training, sales promotion and practical selling; basic research, including audience research and market data; company organization and policies.

Knowledge is but one requirement for success. A sales manager must also have the ability to:

1) Analyze advertising trends so that a station's sales plans will benefit therefrom.

2) Stimulate the sales team so that the most efficient, effective sales effort is applied.

3) Coordinate service functions of the department for accurate and economical operation.

4) Handle in-person presentations to all levels of advertisers.

5) Organize, direct and maintain a proper and efficient method of communications between all members of the sales and management team. The accurate and immediate flow of information is vital to the effectiveness of an independent station's sales organization.

With these requirements in mind, perhaps the best way to illustrate the role of the independent station sales manager is to examine closely his relationship to the other department heads of the management team.

General Manager's Relationship

The most critical aspect of this relationship exists in the establishment of a proper rate structure. The sales manager should have immediately accessible all information concerning the competition within his marketing area and, in addition, be well advised concerning the operations of other stations in similar marketing areas. Then, in association with the general manager, the sales manager should initiate sales plans which will most effectively sell the station's basic commodity—60-second announcements—at the highest possible rate consistent with the station audience performance.

In many instances the sales manager can influence the general manager to establish special-project programming which will fulfill a sales need, bearing in mind constantly that such programming, to be effective and lasting, must provide real appeal to the viewers and value to the client. Examples of this type of sales-program planning are the KTTV Sports Package, initiated four years ago, and the Special Events Package, initiated seven years ago. Both plans provide for a set schedule of events on a monthly basis, and additionally include an "escrow fund" provided by the advertiser to allow the station to take advantage of "last minute" program opportunities—an area in which the properly managed independent can move with speed and resourcefulness. Indeed, the world of an independent is one of flexibility, constantly changing (not always the case with networks or most of their affiliates), and when an opportunity is seen it must be seized.

Finally, the sales manager must consistently provide the intelligence from the market place so that the general manager can, within reason, accurately project revenues against cost and therefore adequately plan for future program development and promotion.

PROGRAM DIRECTOR'S RELATIONSHIP

Many of the sales manager's functions with regard to the general manager are performed in concert with the program director. As a matter of fact, a sales-oriented program director is the greatest asset a sales manager can have. However, let me say to program directors everywhere, who are constantly plagued by us "program oriented" sales managers: "Stand up for your position." If it were not for the program director's judgment, consistency of performance and ability to say "no" for the station's good, station operations might be dictated entirely by commercial opportunity without the balance of public need.

The sales manager should consult regularly with the program manager regarding the sales potential of the program schedule (actual and proposed) and the programs' personalities. Conversely, he should keep the Program Department apprised of sponsors' preferences and recommendations concerning new programs and types of programs.

The intelligence function of an industry-oriented sales manager is extremely important in his relationship with the program director. Having immediate access to program information from all markets by his contact with agencies, advertisers, other stations and, in some cases, producers, he should be in a position to spot specific trends as they develop.

CHIEF ENGINEER

The sales manager consults with the chief engineer concerning client inquiries and requirements that relate to engineering facilities. He himself should be thoroughly familiar with all of his own engineering patterns as well as those of his competitors.

PUBLICITY AND PROMOTION DIRECTOR

In selling an independent, the support of a strong Publicity and Promotion Department is most necessary. In the critical balance between profit and loss there can be no sins of omission, and it is in this area most independent stations are neglectful. An efficiently-run, cost-conscious Publicity and Promotion Department can add a great deal of spice to the selling, as well as to the performance, of an independent.

LEGAL DEPARTMENT

The sales manager must constantly fight the desire for higher returns at the expense of station integrity. This is particularly true in the case of an independent in a major market where the opportunity for additional revenue from marginal local advertising exists abundantly. An independent operation can be as truly judged by the advertising it does not accept as by the business it does take. As a matter of policy it is wise for the Sales Department to maintain a close working contact with the Legal Department, and in the same vein, with the Continuity Acceptance Department. The dollar lost today by avoiding the pitfalls of marginal advertising will pay off in greater gains at a later date.

BUSINESS MANAGER

Through his intelligence system, the sales manager must be alert to bad credit risks, marginal trade deals, and get-well-quick schemes that are offered, in varying ways, by sharp local (and a few national) agencies and clients. It's delightful to bring in that $100,-000 annual sale from a local dealer, but when he's into you for half that amount it ceases to be funny. In a major market this can happen rapidly; only by close communication between the Sales Department and the business manager can this be prevented.

MERCHANDISING MANAGER

Merchandising is a much maligned word, carelessly used by many second or third rate stations to justify inefficient media values. Depending upon the market situation, a strong Merchandising Department (again with a careful eye to efficiency) can often be the difference between a sale or its loss. However, to be effective, merchandising must be practical. From the media standpoint it has only one objective: to assist and stimulate the movement of the client's goods off the shelves—in other words, *to sell*. Jumbo post cards or telephone calls are not in themselves meaningful. A Merchandising Department should be a planned, functional operation with an established list of services, constantly in action and available to all clients who need it. An outstanding example of a well-conceived merchandising program is that established at KTTV by Jack O'Mara (now Vice President of TVB). It has been consistently singled out by national advertisers as one of the best media merchandising programs of its kind. The ingredients are control, applicable market knowledge, intelligent implementation (help where help is needed, not duplicating the job that the client should do himself) and *results*.

The wise independent sales manager will look for a way to provide real sales, in addition to media values, for his clients through effective merchandising programs.

RESEARCH AND SALES

No longer can we underestimate the basic value of audience research as a primary sales tool, particularly for national advertisers. Much has been said lately about the vagaries of the research services that are available to us. While their methods leave something to be desired, they are the best we have and with intelligent application can prove very useful. This is particularly true for the independent who, facing critical competition from the networks, must continually sell his position in the market and provide specialized advertising opportunities not otherwise available. Because of favorable pricing and the ability to deliver the longer commercial in prime time, the independent can justifiably present a strong case for a good portion of all budgets allocated for his market. Qualified research is the tool that proves this and so should be used extensively.

In most instances, the Research Department of an independent will not fall under the direct supervision of the sales manager. Therefore, a thorough understanding between the sales manager and the research director is required to the effect that there will be:

1) Continuing analysis of competitive programming.
2) Continuing analysis of the special programming of one's own station.
3) Analysis of advertising schedules placed on the competition for comparison with the original goals the agency and advertiser had in mind. If these goals are not being properly fulfilled this should be called to the client's attention and a switch proposal, meeting his needs, should be made.
4) Continuing analysis of CPM delivered by competing stations for distribution to all sales executives. Sales personnel must be kept up to date on other stations' rates so that they can intelligently meet *this* competition.
5) Immediate break-out of Broadcast Advertisers Reports that detail advertisers' buys on competing stations.

In the area of over-all planning, the Research Department can analyze the cost-per-thousand-homes situation of competitive programming, and thereby assist the sales manager in determining his own pricing. On a day-to-day basis, the Research Department is a valuable aid in helping the sales personnel of an independent prove the additional reach and advertising frequency it can add to advertisers' campaigns.

Importance of the Traffic Department

At an independent station, perhaps more than at others, the Traffic Department represents central control, for it is here that:

1) Commercial availabilities are dispatched to all sales personnel. (These "logs" should easily reflect what is available for sale now, and what will be available at future dates. Information about special situations should be transmitted by memo locally and by TWX to the national representative.)
2) Orders are received and processed from the national sales offices and from local salesmen.
3) Confirmations are sent out and necessary substitutions are made.
4) A daily inventory report is prepared for the sales manager so that he can balance and control sales requirements between national and local sales.

As was stated before, one of the essentials in the Sales Department of an independent is flexibility. This is nowhere more true than in the case of a major market independent. It is this flexibility, particularly to accommodate local sales, that tends to complicate the operation of the Traffic Department. The jockeying for positions between local salesmen themselves as well as between local and national sales can create a situation of chaos and inefficency. The Traffic Department should be under the direct supervision of the sales manager so that he can control his inventory as he sees fit and for the station's best interest, maintaining the essential flexibility. (See Chapter 16 for a more detailed discussion—Ed.)

THE LOCAL SALES TEAM

An independent station has a responsibility not only to the community it serves, but also to the merchants and manufacturers within that community. It should maintain a balanced commercial schedule that will provide for the local or regional advertiser the opportunity to utilize the television medium. In determining what this balance (or ratio of national to local business) should be, market size and location will probably be the determining factors. In the case of Los Angeles, the balance will more often be 50/50 and never swing more than 60/40 either way. In smaller markets, the balance will favor the national side.

Because local and regional business are so important to the independent, a great deal of attention must be given to the sales staff and the way it is utilized. A small but highly professional local sales force compensated by a minimum weekly guarantee against an attractive incentive structure is the best arrangement. A group like this are, in effect, almost independent contractors. In major markets, good local salesmen will earn from $20,000 to $30,000 a year. This system tends to result in a professional, proficient, highly skilled sales staff that value their jobs and guard them jealously. The sales manager, of course, must determine the number of skilled salesmen required to handle his estimated or projected local billing. At KTTV, billing between $4,000,000 and $5,000,000 annually from local and regional advertisers, we operate with never less than five nor more than six salesmen.

Despite incentives, salesmen are transitory. The aggressive salesman always is looking for management opportunity. Therefore, it is wise to maintain a pool of young men (sales assistants) who are ready to move up when an opportunity presents itself. By having these assistants perform some clerical duties, it is economically possible to afford them. Furthermore, a young, aggressive potential replacement can be a powerful psychological stimulant to an older, well-compensated salesman. At KTTV, this system has proved most effective; in four years it has given us six highly competent, thoroughly trained salesmen who filled vacancies immediately without requiring six months to a year of training. We now have two assistants for five salesmen.

The sales manager must distribute his manpower so that each local salesman has potentially the same sales opportunity. Agencies develop personalities and while it is true that a good salesman should be able to cope with all situations, one salesman will often be able to handle a given agency better than another. For efficiency in sales, attention must be paid to this factor. Agency assignments should be made subject to regular six-month reviews. Personal relationships can help sales. They also can damage the sales effort. Do not hesitate to make changes. There are times when "change just for change's sake" is good and keeps the salesmen stimulated and on their toes.

Reporting is essential, but should be kept to a minimum. A salesman bogged down with unnecessary reporting cannot be on the street doing his primary job. However, these are not nine-to-five workers and they should be required to provide all the sales information the sales manager deems necessary.

General sales meetings should be held at least once a week. These should be well planned in advance so that they do not take an inordinate amount of time. Plan at these meetings for an interchange of market and sales information so that each salesman can benefit from others' experience in the market place.

It is a good idea to assign each local salesman as a specialist on a competing station. It should be his responsibility to have a complete knowledge and understanding of its programming, policies, rate card and especially any deviations from that rate card.

The sales manager should stimulate competition among his salesmen while maintaining balance. At KTTV, which for years was generally conceded to have one of the best local sales staffs in the major western markets, the competition was often keener among the salesmen than between the competing stations. This was not done with contests, prizes or other gimmicks; a good commission structure and pride have been enough stimulus.

It is also important for the sales manager to encourage and stimulate creativity. This is the strongest single asset a local independent salesman can have. In local market selling, highly competitive (wholesale) CPM's can often be overcome by a strong creative idea.

Finally, a general sales manager and his local sales manager should back up their men strongly, even in the case of mistakes if they are honestly and infrequently made. But be sure that it is clear that they do not make the same mistake again. A strong salesman will take advantage of any opportunity to increase his billing. Judgment and control must be properly exercised to prevent him from doing that at the station's expense. At the same time such control must be exercised without damaging his enthusiasm or aggressiveness.

Insofar as prices are concerned, the sales manager should maintain the same rate structure for both national and local advertisers. If there is a quality product and it is fairly priced, there is no justification for dual rates. In independent television the temptations are strong to favor the "bird in the hand." Experience (and some regrets) have proved that this is wrong. Television has now proved itself the most powerful selling medium extant and within the broad spectrum of the medium, the well managed independent station is fulfilling a real service. Priced fairly, and with the additional services it can provide, there is no need for wild discounting of availabilities still existing as the day they are available draws near. When our product is not sold commercially it still has real value to the station for promotional purposes. It should not be arbitrarily wholesaled just to pick up the last dollar. Whenever this happens the station's entire rate structure will seek this lower level.

NATIONAL REPRESENTATIVE

The position of the national representative in television has been undergoing radical change during the past few years. These years have seen NBC and CBS Spot Sales confining that activity to just the o and o's. ABC Spot Sales is formed to do the same thing, and the growth of the group-owned representative such as Metro TV

Sales (Metro Broadcast-Television), TVAR (Westinghouse), Storer, RKO General, and others further changes the picture.

There are two basic reasons for this proliferation: 1) The over-all national sales volume generated by the groups as a whole is sufficient to underwrite national sales costs at a rate equal to or less than that which must be charged by the national representative; 2) a more efficient, creative and thorough sales job can be done by a man representing just a few stations than by a man whose company expects him to represent 20 or even more stations.

Prior to its sale to Metromedia, KTTV determined that it had enough national sales volume to open its own offices in New York, Chicago and San Francisco, thus becoming the first major independent set up to handle its own national sales efforts. In approximately 45 weeks of operation, this effort resulted in a 40% increase in national billing over the previous year at a most efficient cost-to-sales ratio.

In choosing the representative, bear in mind the principles outlined above. Examine the company closely at the management level. Find out how many stations they are set up to handle. How many do they have now? Are any of their stations similar in programming and market patterns? Is their manpower sufficient as it is now constituted, or will they have to add new personnel to handle another station? What has been their sales record with similar properties? With New York representing 65% of national spot billing, find out how their New York office compares with the representatives of competitors. Once chosen, the successful growth of the station's national sales will depend largely on the sales manager's ability to work closely with his representative firm in directing and stimulating its sales efforts.

The following points, properly executed, should serve to create a good, selling, station-representative relationship.

1) Insist, if at all possible, that each of the representative's salesmen visit the station and market at least once a year, if only for a short time. First-hand knowledge of an independent's market and operating philosophy is vital to its proper representation in major buying areas.

2) By the same token, the sales manager should visit his representative's offices at frequent intervals. There is no substitute

for making actual sales calls with the "rep" salesman. Both benefit tremendously, he from the indirect information imparted during the presentation and the sales manager from the competitive knowledge gained in the free exchange of ideas and sales points with the media buyers.

3) Don't duplicate communications. Have one central point for clearance for all representative dealings so that immediate answers can be received. With western independents, "time difference" is a very important factor in communications. Being 3,000 miles away and with a three-hour time difference, communication can be very frustrating unless strict attention is paid to detail and system.

4) Every effort should be made to clear and confirm sales orders within 48 hours. Efficient operation can expedite the rep's selling relationships with his agencies.

5) When an order is confirmed—back it up! See that it runs as ordered. Nothing is more damaging to the national sales effort than a sloppily run independent that causes the rep to keep plaguing the agencies with a constant stream of booking errors, pre-emptions after the fact, or billing errors. After one bad experience, the buyer will say, "Who needs it?!"

6) As with the local sales staff, it is even more important that the national representative be backed up. A smart, well-run representative, thoroughly informed concerning the station and its market, will add immeasurably to the station's prestige and *sales*.

7) As in the case of the local Sales Department, excessive reporting takes time away from the principal selling function. However, the rep should be prepared to provide all details on business lost (reason why, competitive offering, CPM, etc.). Filed along with the original availability request and eventual submission, these provide the basis for "switch pitches" later on.

8) The sales manager should see that he is provided with copies of all availability requests from all national offices. From these he can contact local representatives (brokers, agents or company executives), informing them of the pending campaign and enlisting their support on behalf of his station. An independent, under heavy competition, should always try to maintain a close and continuing contact with the "field" men of

national clients. These men are on the scene and can be expected to report to the home office the exact standing of the station in the community and the value of any additional services it may perform. "Selling in depth" of this kind is often the difference between winning and losing.

SUMMARY

The goal of the sales manager is obvious: increasing sales. But the techniques for accomplishing this are much more involved. In the final analysis, the requirements prominently include the utilization of all of a station's facilities to provide the best possible commercial availabilities for the client, while being sure that professional local and national salesmen are fully aware of these availabilities and their advantages, and that they carry this information persuasively to the right clients at the right time.

These functions are different for the independent television station for several reasons. Generally the competition of an independent station is formidable, for it includes the expensive and impressive array of network programming. On the other hand, the independent has the advantage of being able to program with more versatility to its market and for its clients. It can also make available more minute commercials in the prime nighttime hours. It can offer commercial and programming sponsorships that are inherently efficient, and can also provide availabilities that are efficient in supplementing the reach and frequency of campaigns on other stations. It is the task of the sales manager to harness his station's advantages to overcome the aggressiveness of his independent competitors and offset the powerhouse programming of the network stations in his market. It's a tough job. But it definitely can be done.

CHAPTER 15

The National
Sales Representative

BY JOHN B. SIAS

Metromedia, Inc., New York

A graduate of Stanford University where he majored in economics, Mr. Sias learned about the work of a national sales representative in the newspaper business and then in the television firm of Peters, Griffin and Woodward in Chicago, New York and San Francisco where he was Vice President for television for the west coast. Mr. Sias was later associated with Westinghouse Broadcasting Company as National Television Sales Manager before joining Metromedia, Inc. in 1963 as Vice President and Director of Metro TV Sales.

THE largest source of a station's revenue is that produced by the national sales representative, the sales force of the television station for sales originating outside its home market. The system developed in the television field in 1948, when established national radio representatives started to set up separate television sales organizations in anticipation of big investments by advertisers in national spot television.

At the present time there are more than 30 television representative organizations. They can be divided into two distinct classifications: those that are independently owned and those that are owned by broadcasting companies.

Among the independent television representatives are such major organizations as: Blair TV; Edward Petry; Harrington-Righter & Parsons; Peters, Griffin, Woodward; Katz; H-R Reps; George P. Hollingbery; Young-TV; Advertising Time Sales.

Company-owned representatives are the sales representative

arm of the stations (or networks) and include such as these: ABC National Spot Sales; CBS-TV Stations' National Sales; Crosley Sales; Metro TV Sales; NBC-TV Spot Sales; RKO General National Sales; Storer Television Sales; TVAR.

The volume of national spot advertising is dramatically revealed in the fact that the business written by these organizations, other smaller independent representatives, and the New York and Chicago television stations was more than $541 million in 1962.

The national sales representatives will typically maintain offices in the principal advertising centers so that they can work directly and closely with the advertising agencies and clients headquartered in those cities. There they act as the sales agents and principal sources of information about the stations they represent. The percentage of total national spot dollars coming from these major advertising centers is as follows:

Estimated Percentage of Total National Spot Originations*

New York	65%
Chicago	20%
San Francisco	4%
Los Angeles	4%
St. Louis	2%
Atlanta	2%
Detroit	1%
All other	2%

* Source: FCC National Report—Station Revenue, August 1963.

Individual station percentages will vary greatly depending on the location of the station. For example, a Los Angeles station will tend to have a much higher percentage of national spot revenue from San Francisco and a lesser percentage from Chicago. A Minneapolis station will have a minimal amount of its total national spot volume from the west coast, but will have a heavy amount from Chicago.

As would be expected, the distribution of national representative manpower has a relationship to the size of the dollar potential in the markets listed above. New York, in almost every case, is the headquarters of the representative. It is here, generally speaking, that the company will maintain a sales staff twice as large as that in Chicago. Regional offices depend on the size of the representative organization; usually such offices have just one or two men, with secretaries. The larger national representatives, both independent and company-owned, have between 20 and 40 spot-time salesmen or account executives selling for the station they represent. In addition to account executives/salesmen, each representative firm maintains specialists in areas of importance to the stations, such as: research, promotion, sales development, and traffic. Still other specialists may concentrate on selling special program events, public service programs, and/or other locally originated programming. Such programs are currently being produced in greater profusion by individual and group stations.

METHODS OF OPERATION

Television stations sell announcements of varying lengths such as 60 seconds, 20 seconds, 8 or 10 seconds, as well as complete programs. Of the $541 million spent in spot television by national advertisers in 1962, 11% went for program sponsorship and 89% went to announcements. This kind of "inventory" is rather unique. It is unlike a manufacturer's in that once a given time is passed, that portion of inventory occupying it and unsold, is lost forever to the station. Furthermore, there is a limit to the number of announcements that are available to take care of a demand for items such as any specific adjacencies to news programs or high-rated evening programs.

The national representative, to be effective in dealing with this perishable inventory, must have speedy and accurate hour-by-hour communication with the television stations for whom he works. Agency buyers want to know from the national representative what announcements are available for purchase during the period when a television schedule is planned to run. They further must know rates for announcements, details on program personalities, station coverage, merchandising plans available, and other related information that will transform their clients' investments on a television station into a productive expenditure.

The national representative assigns salesmen or account executives to each agency. An agency will call its assigned salesman for any information it wants on his represented stations. As an example, a Chicago advertising agency seeking to place a schedule of 60-second nighttime announcements in the New York market would contact, in writing or by phone, the representatives of the six New York stations. The agency would request that by a certain date the stations must submit their proposed availabilities of the type desired, in this case 60 seconds, to the agency for its consideration. The respective salesmen assigned to the agency would consult their Traffic Departments and availability sheets for a proposed schedule. In all probability they double-check with the station sales manager, apprising him of the up-coming business and requesting suggestions from him as to what should or should not be offered.

A written presentation would then be prepared by the account executive and his sales secretary. This presentation would typically include the time periods being offered, program adjacencies, audience information, ratings and homes. In some cases, audience information will include a breakdown of men, women, and/or children viewing the commercial time periods. Also included will be costs per announcement, package costs, and suggested schedules. The enterprising national representative will attempt to sell other elements of station value beyond the schedule of announcements he is offering in his sales presentation. In this way the buyer will be reminded of advantages not offered by one of the competing stations in the market. The representative will attempt to know and convey rating histories, up-coming programming, special promotion that will be run by his station, merchandising assistance that might be available to this client and other facts which commend the buy to the agency purchaser.

Typically the account executive will make a personal presentation. During this presentation an effort will be made to secure an order then and there. Announcements that are so attractive that they are particularly susceptible to prior sale will be pushed. However, a buy is not usually made when the initial presentation is submitted. In such cases, the representative salesman continues to maintain personal and/or phone contact with the buyer and others whom he feels have an influence on the sale until the schedule is obtained or lost.

Assuming the commercial schedule that was submitted is ordered, the station representative will telephone or TWX the specifics of the order to the station and ask for confirmation of the availability of those announcements which have been ordered. It is then that the station Traffic Department and/or general manager must decide if they can clear all announcements ordered. If some have been sold, substitutes will be offered to the buyer as alternatives. The entire process, to be successful, entails a combination of persistence, persuasiveness, and a close attention to the myriad of details involved.

Literally hundreds of millions of dollars of such commercial positions, called "spot television," are purchased each year by means of verbal orders which frequently are not followed by written contracts until after schedules have started to run. In such a relationship, it is of the utmost importance that the representative be well-informed concerning his stations, that he be honest with his buyers, and be accurate in his work.

When the representative receives written confirmation from the station that the schedule has been set up as ordered, a formal

ELEVISION CONFIRMATION ND CONTRACT

Metro Broadcast Sales
A SERVICE OF METROPOLITAN BROADCASTING

OFFICE...:...,.........................,........

SALESMAN.....:........................

DATE ....

STATION..............................

ADVERTISER..........................

PRODUCT ....

DAY	TIME	TYPE	CLASS	FREQUENCY OR SEC. PLAN	EARNED RATE	CARD#

ARTING DATE	EXPIRATION DATE	CONTRACT YEAR	TYPE OF ORDER	NO. OF WEEKS	
			NEW ☐ RENEWAL ☐		LIVE ☐ FILM ☐ TAPE ☐ SLIDE ☐

ARTING ATE CARD	FUTURE RATE CARD	BILLING METHOD	WEEKLY	TOTAL CONTRACT
	NO. MO. DAY YEAR	AS EARNED ☐ END OF FREQUENCY ☐ BLANKET ☐		

agency commission unless otherwise noted. Subject to station's standard broadcasting conditions on the back hereof and any special conditions set forth above or attached hereto.

............................,..............   ....••

CEPTED FOR AGENCY   ACCEPTED FOR STATION

contract is prepared with copies sent to both the agency and the station.

Even after a sale is made most schedules require constant representative service. Television representatives must keep the buyers apprised regarding program changes affecting the schedule, rate changes that may affect the costs, changes in levels of audience at time periods that have been purchased which would affect the efficiency of the buy. During these complex and seemingly endless negotiations the national spot representative is, to all intent and purpose, the station in the eyes of the time buyer. If the representative is diligent in attending to the details and service required by the account, and is accurate and prompt in his paper work, the station benefits. Conversely, a good station can be hurt by an inefficient performance by its representative.

Television representatives, to be successful, must have from their represented stations a fast and complete flow of accurate information. Most large representatives give their sales staff proper supporting material and facts through several departments.

THE PROMOTION DEPARTMENT

The Promotion Department obtains from stations information about their programs, rates, audience size, coverage, and matters of advertising benefit. It will correlate this material and organize it into files that the sales staff can use. These files will contain sales success stories, program schedules, merchandising plans, coverage data, and other information of interest to the advertising agency buyer. The Promotion Department also often works with the station's sales managers and their promotion manager to develop special sales presentations about the various stations or markets.

THE TRAFFIC DEPARTMENT

The rapid tempo and the in-and-out character of national spot sales makes inventory control essential. The representative must have up-to-the-minute details on what is and what is not available on all stations whose time he sells. To facilitate accurate information about what is available for sale, many large representatives maintain hourly contact via TWX and telephone with their represented stations. Their Traffic Department marks off as no longer available announcements or programs as they are sold, or posts them as available when there is a cancellation. Traffic keeps up to date an availability board that is the control point in the representative's New York office for what the sales staff can reasonably expect to sell and clear if an order is obtained. The Traffic Department attempts to keep these logs for each station and provide the sales staff with availabilities on a regular basis.

All orders must be confirmed in writing. *Time is of the essence.* Therefore, TWX is the basic form of written communication between representatives and stations on all matters pertaining to schedules. It is fast. It leaves a permanent record. The Traffic Department is in charge of TWXing all schedules ordered. Further, it is in charge of getting back to an individual salesman with incoming messages from stations concerning changes in schedules, programming, rates, etc. Most Traffic Departments have a standard TWX form for ordering schedules. The Traffic Department in its importance to national spot sales is often likened to the underwater portion of an iceberg. It is little seen outside the organization,

TWX ORDER FORM

O: _____ DATE: _____
  (contact)   (call letters) (mkt.)

M: _____ TIME: _____
  (salesman)   MTVS   (office)

E: _____
  (account) (product) (agency)   (time buyer)

RATING SERVICE:

HAVE SOLD THE FOL SKED TO START _____ FOR _____
                   (date)   (length)

THRU _____ AS FOL
  (end date)

LIST SKED HERE:

       N.B. Be sure to list per spot cost unless Major Coverage Plan or other where we do not quote a per spot price.

however, although it is deeply involved in every sales transaction. It can help the sales staff and station obtain extra orders through its proper functioning. On the other hand, through ineptitude or lassitude it can cost dearly in lost sales and poor customer relations. (See Chapter 16 for a detailed discussion.—Ed.)

THE RESEARCH DEPARTMENT

The increasing use of vastly more detailed audience figures by buyers has caused many representatives to establish large Research Departments. These departments are in charge of arming the sales representatives with such information as detailed ratings histories and trends on specific programs, audience composition data, basic market facts, and insights into weaknesses of competitive stations. The Research Departments further attempt to put into quickly useable form the periodic audience reports received by a station. From time to time, they will undertake, depending on the representative and the stations involved, special research projects. If the past is any guide, it is apparent that the Research Department will become a more important part of the national sales representative operations as more and more audience data are put into use by the buyers.

STATION COUNSELING

It is not surprising that the national representative is frequently looked to by his station customers for counsel or recommendations on matters pertaining to programming, rates, research, promotion, and even personnel. In many cases, a periodic general review session is held with the stations' executives. These reviews will include examinations of audience trends, the present station sales performance, pricing analyses, and estimated shares of national business. Depending on the situation, specific recommendations may include a program change, a new rate card, and/or ideas on sales promotion. If necessary, personnel changes may be recommended. There are other instances where these matters are discussed informally. The point is that the national representative is so important to the station's total revenue picture, he exercises a profound, albeit indirect influence on the course of many station operations. The role of counselor or advisor that is present in many situations appears to have increased in recent years, and it is predicted by many that it will continue to grow as the business becomes more complex.

COMPENSATION

Television stations generally compensate their representatives on a commission basis, a system dating back to the early days of radio. Under this system, the station pays a stated commission on every dollar of business brought in by the representative office. There was a time when the representative received 15%, the same commission as paid to advertising agencies; but, with some notable exceptions, a 15% commission rate for television representatives is not common now. Commission contracts currently range from a low of 5% to as much as 15%, with the majority appearing to fall within the area of 7½% to 10%.

There are two types of commission contracts. One is a flat commission basis for all national business sold by the representative. The second method is a graduated commission rate which may go up or down depending on the individual station-representative arrangement. As an example, in those going up, a commission of 8% might be paid on a given quota of business; a higher rate of commission, such as a 9% or 10%, might be paid on all business sold beyond that quota. In a descending contract, a commission of 10% might be given for a certain amount of business; a lower rate would be given for a greater amount of business, and an even lower rate for business beyond that, according to the contract involved.

The development of self representation by group operators, accompanied by the rapid growth of total national spot dollars, appears to have put pressure on the commission rates charged by representatives in the major markets. As a general rule, larger market stations will pay a lower commission rate than the smaller market stations. Commission rates are spelled out in the station-representative contract; these contracts further stipulate that geographical area from which the representative will sell the station and that which will be covered by the station's own sales staff. Station representative contracts generally cover a one year or two year period. Most contracts stipulate that a notice of intent to cancel must be given in advance. Ninety days to one year appears to be the generally accepted range for this. If such notice is not given, the contract is usually automatically renewed.

SUMMARY

Such is the world of the national sales representative, the sales force that is responsible for the greatest part of a television station's advertising revenue. Representation itself is a professional, personal, service business. The representative's effectiveness is greatly dependent upon the relationship between representative and station—a relationship that should express mutual trust, respect, and wholehearted cooperation so as to assure maximum sales results.

CHAPTER 16

Traffic Management
for Sales

BY NORMAN ZIEGLER

A graduate of Boston University, Mr. Ziegler entered broadcasting in 1957 through the mailroom of WHDH-AM-FM-TV in Boston, Massachusetts, and was soon promoted to Assistant National Television Sales Manager where he learned the intricacies of station traffic. Mr. Ziegler subsequently left broadcasting for the advertising business, and he is currently on the other side of the fence (or screen) as an advertising agency television time buyer.

SALES activity at a television station creates such voluminous detail that a Traffic Department is necessary for the control and dissemination of this information. This department also reports all operational detail and so is important to virtually every other department of the station, to the networks of those stations that are affiliated, and to advertising agencies.

THE PROGRAM LOG

At every television station the basic tool of operation is the daily program schedule from sign-on to sign-off or, as it is more commonly termed, the program log. The log is the composite of the mass of programming, production and commercial information and material provided by the network, by agencies and by the station. The role of the traffic manager is to coordinate this information and to prepare the log.

The log contains the chronological order and timing, to the split second, of all programs (local and network), of all commercials, and of all promotional and public service announcements. Further, it provides origination information for all programming:

that is, whether a program, commercial or non-commercial announcement is local or network; color or black and white; live, film, slide or videotape. In addition, the log indicates the time to switch from network programming to local programming and vice versa, as well as when to cut away from the network for local station breaks. Finally, the log is the permanent record of the station's broadcast day, and must be kept on file as required by the FCC.

The traffic (program) log is used by every major division of the television station. It is the schedule the engineers in the control room literally use to push the buttons for the day's telecasting. With the log in front of him, the engineer knows when to switch to and from the network, when to start the film projectors for programs and announcements, and when to set in motion the videotape machines and slide projectors. In short, using the log as his only authority, the engineer in the master control room is responsible for maintaining the proper order of all programming throughout the broadcast day.

Every day, a copy of the log for the next day's broadcasting is sent to the Film Department. From this, the film editors prepare the reels of announcements, insert film commercials into film programs, and set up slide trays in correct sequence. Producers and directors of local programs depend on the log to know how many and what announcements are scheduled in their programs, and the exact timing and origination of these announcements. Finally, the log is the only source used by the Accounting Department to bill the station's advertisers. Should any billing problem arise (such as a missed announcement) the log is the final authority to which to refer.

Clearly, the program log is the backbone of the station's day-to-day operation. The variety of important functions it performs reflects the complexity of television station operation and the dependence of each department on the other. The myriad of detail involved in the preparation of the log, and the accuracy of the information in it, are the direct responsibility of the traffic manager.

The Network and the Traffic Manager

In the case of those stations affiliated with or owned by a network, there is considerable contact between the network and the traffic manager. From the network comes program information, conveyed by the program director, and commercial information which is communicated directly. Network information includes the weekly schedule of network programs, as well as cues and timings indicating when station breaks will occur in and between network programs. Information is also provided to keep the traffic manager abreast of any interruptions or pre-emptions expected in the regular network program schedule. When special programs or news events pre-empt regular shows the traffic manager must note the change and, if local station commercials are affected by the change, the Sales Department must be informed.

From the network's commercial information the traffic manager learns what advertisers are sponsoring which programs, and the exact timings for the network commercials. These data are especially important so as to preclude the scheduling of local station announcements too close to a network announcement advertising a similar product—known as "product conflict." To avoid this problem, the traffic manager records all network information on an "availability sheet," the record (revised weekly) of what times and positions are available for sale by the station in and between network and local programs.

In some instances a network commercial will require a local station tag. For example, a clothing advertiser on a network program may want to tell viewers in a city where, in that city, his product can be purchased. The network, then, will advise the traffic desk of the exact moment the station is to cut away from the commercial and schedule the local dealer or store tag.

All together, network information concerning the scheduling of programs, commercials, and local tags represents the primary relationship between the station's Traffic Department and that station's network.

SCHEDULING COMMERCIALS AND ANNOUNCEMENTS

In its contact with the advertising agencies, the Traffic Department is primarily concerned with the scheduling of commercials. When a station has perhaps 100 accounts on the air, and each advertiser has two, four, or a dozen different commericals he wishes to use, the amount of commercial material received by the Traffic Department often reaches staggering proportions. For example, a 52-week advertiser may rotate five different 20-second commercials through his schedule, then may change his campaign and use 10-second slides, and then revert to 20-second spots. Or an advertiser running a short three- or four-week saturation campaign may use five or six different commercials, each of which is to be followed by a dealer tag. Furthermore, it is not uncommon for an agency to call the Traffic Department with a last minute schedule change in film rotation. On top of all this, every agency has a different system of instructions and each account requires special handling. Therefore, the Traffic Department must maintain accurate records and a foolproof coding system. Any mistakes can cost the station money through missed or incorrect commercials.

The station's Program Department, of course, schedules all programming during the hours when the network does not broadcast. While there is little variance in day-to-day local programming, the changes that do occur must be communicated promptly by the traffic manager so that they can be reflected on the availability sheet and on the log.

The Promotion/Publicity Department makes constant demands on the traffic manager by requesting availabilities for the great many non-commercial announcements telecast daily by the station. All unsold positions are filled with station promotion spots for local or network programs, and with public service announcements. In the latter case, the traffic manager generally is given the material, films, and/or slides and copy to be used. Most stations' budgets do not allow for a public service director, so it is the traffic manager who does this scheduling and he must keep appropriate records. Similarly, the traffic manager generally does the scheduling of the local and network promotional announcements, and keeps these records. And, of course, all of these announcements that are on film must, like the commercial announcements, be coded for use by the film editors.

SALES DEPARTMENT RELATIONSHIP

It is the Sales Department, however, that makes the most demands on the traffic manager's time and abilities. With all network and local programming as well as network commercial data recorded on the availability sheet, the traffic manager is now prepared to handle the most important phase of his job—receiving and processing orders for sales of station time. It is the job of the salesmen to sell all available time. It is the job of the traffic manager to insure that the salesmen know at all times exactly how much time and what positions are available for sale. With as many as 10 local salesmen and the national sales manager all competing for spots, with a minimum of 100 different accounts on the air and new ones coming on daily, and with a fixed number of commercial positions available for sale, the sales aspect of the traffic manager's function is most exacting.

To fully understand the relationship between Sales and Traffic, let us take an order for commercial time and follow it, through the eyes of the traffic manager, from the moment availabilities are requested until the commercial appears on the log. Assume that an agency wishes to order a schedule of announcements for one of its clients. The local salesman or national representative is notified by the agency of the specifics of the campaign; that is, the length of commercial positions desired, the nature of the commercials—whether film, slide, tape, or live—the budget available, and the length of the campaign. The salesman or national sales manager immediately conveys this information to the traffic manager to determine what spot announcements are available to meet the needs of the client. From the availability sheet, the most appropriate spots are selected for consideration by the timebuyer. When the buying decision has been made, the salesman takes the order back to Traffic to order or "book" the spots. If any of the spots ordered have been previously sold by another salesman or another office of the national representative, then the traffic manager must find replacement spots or "makegoods" to resubmit to the agency. When the order is finally confirmed, the spots are recorded on the availability sheet with their starting and expiration dates. After the commercial material has been received, the spot is entered on the log along with its film, slide or tape number. This is the basic operation.

It would be reasonable to assume that, once a schedule has been confirmed, the traffic manager's part in the sales operation would be over. No assumption could be more erroneous. Servicing the account is the next phase of the traffic function. If, for example, the schedule had been ordered for eight weeks and had six spots there would be 48 spots that could potentially be missed, incorrectly telecast or changed for a variety of reasons. These are some of the reasons:

1) *Fixed or pre-emptible spots:*   Many stations have rate cards which allow an advertiser to purchase announcements at different rates. Discount plans vary from station to station but are universal in the industry. Some stations allow a discount on the number of spots run during a 12-month period. For example, if an advertiser ran 26, 52, 104, 156 or more spots during that period, his cost per spot would be lower according to how many spots were run. Other stations discount spots according to the number of spots run each week. Still other stations discount spots if they have been bought on a pre-emptible basis. A 20-second spot can cost $500. However, should an advertiser have a limited budget he can pay less than $500, say $400, if he agrees to the risk that his spot be pre-emptible on two weeks' notice by an advertiser paying the higher rate. Such pre-emptions can be permanent (six weeks out of an eight-week flight) or temporary (once or twice during the eight-week flight). In either case, the traffic manager must advise the salesman that his spot has been pre-empted and must then offer makegood spots for the account. This is usually done in memo form and it is a daily occurrence.

2) *Technical errors:*   As an outgrowth of a station's complex technical operation, there are occasions when spots will be telecast incorrectly or missed completely due to a mechanical failure or human error. A film can break; there can be audio or video difficulty; the wrong film can be telecast—the possibilities are endless. In all of these cases, it is the traffic manager's job to keep the salesmen informed of the errors and to try to find makegoods comparable to the missed spots.

3) *Program pre-emptions:*   Changes in network or local programming often cause spots to be missed. If a spot is scheduled at 8:30 P.M. and the network or the local station schedules a special program from 8:00 to 9:00 P.M., that 8:30 P.M. spot will be pre-empted. Obviously a makegood will be necessary.

4) *Traffic errors:*   Traffic managers are not infallible, although salesmen expect them to be. An incorrect time on the log or an incorrect date on the availability sheet can cause an error. The

wrong film number or a commercial no longer in use also can create makegood situations.

5) *Network changes:* Very often a change in the sponsor of a program will create a product conflict with advertisers in adjacent positions. Should this occur, a permanent replacement will be necessary.

All of these potential problem areas are the direct responsibility of the traffic manager. Furthermore, he must be aware of unexpected cancellations of spots and he must inform salesmen of such new availabilities. Conversely, when an account renews a schedule he must advise that anticipated availabilities will not be forthcoming.

OTHER RESPONSIBILITIES

Aside from the daily complexity and enormous detail work to be done, the traffic manager has other duties to perform and other matters requiring his attention. He must distribute the log, daily, to all station departments in order that all personnel can have immediate knowledge of what is being telecast at any given moment. He must prepare and distribute the availability sheet, weekly, not only to the station salesmen and sales manager but to the various offices of the national representative as well. He must, when scheduling commercials, avoid triple-spotting—that is, running three commercials of more than 20 seconds in length, back-to-back. This is contrary to the code of the National Association of Broadcasters although the rule may not apply to non-member stations. He must avoid overloading programs with commercials or non-commercial announcements. This is a major problem when scheduling spots in feature films or other syndicated film programs. Again, the NAB prescribes the number of announcements which can be scheduled and the traffic manager must adhere to these limitations.

Small wonder, then, that the traffic desk at most stations is called "the hot seat." It is the crossroads of every phase of the station operation. The amount of detail is tremendous, and the constant flow of material and information makes errors inevitable. It is demanded of the traffic manager that these errors be as few as possible. The job, clearly, is not an easy one. It requires a great degree of patience, a mind capable of organizing great masses of detail and, most important of all, the ability to deal effectively with people. The problems of salesmen, the phone calls from all departments, and the inevitable meetings are without end. Through all of this, the traffic manager is expected to have all the answers.

From this discussion, it may appear that the traffic manager is the most important person in the station. Obviously such is not the case. In very few industries is the interdependence of departments and personnel more essential than at a television station.

PART FIVE

*TECHNICAL SERVICES AND
MANAGEMENT*

CHAPTER 17

The Engineering Department and its Work

BY SIDNEY V. STADIG

KYW-TV, Group W Stations, Cleveland, Ohio

A native of Natick, Massachusetts, Mr. Stadig began his broadcasting career with the Westinghouse Group W's Boston station, WBZ. Following three years of active service with the Navy during World War II, he rejoined Group W and held managerial television engineering assignments in Boston, Philadelphia and San Francisco before moving to Cleveland in 1956 as Chief Engineer of Westinghouse Broadcasting Company's Group W stations KYW, KYW-FM and KYW-TV. Mr. Stadig is a member of the Society of Motion Picture and Television Engineers and the Institute of Electrical and Electronic Engineers.

THE technical facilities of a television station, and its Engineering Department, are of direct concern for every employee. While it might be thought that this is a self-evident fact, the work of the Engineering Department and its importance to the station's over-all operation are not always fully understood—nor, in some cases, appreciated.

Essentially, the objective of the Engineering Department is to originate and transmit the finest quality signal to the largest possible audience, limited only by restrictions specified in the Federal Communications Commission license and by good judgment regarding capital investment in the technical plant.

The department is directed by the chief engineer (or engineering manager or director of engineering—the title may vary from one station to the next) who is directly responsible to the general manager. On the table of organization chart, his status is equivalent to the department heads for sales, programming, publicity and promotion, and business affairs. The chief engineer must provide operating personnel of the highest possible technical caliber, as well as the necessary plant equipment.

PERSONNEL REQUIREMENTS

One of the most challenging tasks in administering the Engineering Department is to find technical personnel who can *operate* as well as maintain the electronic complexities in a station.

In some stations, program or non-technical people will perform the video switching functions, or will operate studio cameras. Actually, there is some merit in this type of operation. In other stations these job functions are performed by technical personnel—provided that the technical people have the creative or artistic "flair" required to enhance the program as it is being produced.

A cameraman must have an "aptitude" in dollying or panning a camera. He must know picture composition and framing. The same applies to the video switcher or audio console man. There is a *right* instant in switching from one camera to another; otherwise the transition can become a distraction that interrupts the continuity of a story. Similarly, the man on the audio console must have an ear for music and a feel for the audio balance in a program. In each of these assignments, the aptitude to be part and parcel of a program is of the first priority, but technical know-how should materially help to achieve greater finesse. An individual possessing these attributes should be known as a "programmeer" even though he may work under the Engineering Department.*

The complete studio production comes under the direction of a program director or producer who, in turn, directs all of the personnel participating on set as well as the activities behind the scenes. The end product will be contributed to, or impaired by, any one of a number of people required to produce a show—stage hands, film editors, audiomen, lighting technicians, boom-pushers, talent, to name just a few. There is not enough time at the beginning or end of a show to give a full list of "credits" to all of those

---

* *The Technique of Television Production* (1961) by Gerald Millerson, and *The Technique of the Sound Studio* (1962) by Alec Nisbett (both Hastings House) are valuable references in this connection—Ed.

who have participated. The audio boom operator, dolly pusher, and script girl are all equally as important to the success of the show.

The job functions assigned to the Technical Department usually include the following: technical director; audio console; mike boom; lighting; maintenance; projection; videotape; video shader; cameramen; transmitter.

Each technician must know the basic over-all plant video and audio system and each piece of equipment in the system, not only to maintain it properly, but to recognize the early signs of an equipment failure and take immediate remedial action.

FINANCIAL REQUIREMENTS AND COST CONTROL

In the next few years, the transition to solid state devices, the development of improved cameras, more practical videotape recorders and other improved facilities as they become available, will continually improve the performance and the reliability of the over-all equipment in a television station.

The chief engineer and his subordinates must keep abreast of these developments and seek all practicable improvements in upgrading the technical facilities within the financial objectives of the station.

The costs incurred by the Engineering Department, in its relation to the station's profit pattern, fall into three basic categories: committed costs, managed costs, and costs incurred in producing the product. Committed costs include such things as rent, taxes, equipment depreciation and insurance. Most of the Engineering Department expenditures come under the designation of managed and/or product costs. Such cost items include: studio-to-transmitter video and audio lines; power for the transmitter; tubes and/or transistors for all studio and transmitting equipment; lamp bulbs for television studio lamps; lamps for all film and slide projectors, and transmitter tower relamping (in some cases, office light bulbs and miscellaneous lamp fixtures). There are also expenditures for the maintenance of equipment (including spare parts replacements), for the maintenance of the building and grounds, for janitorial services required, and for the operation and maintenance of air-conditioning equipment. Other costs are necessary for replacement of image orthicon and vidicon camera tubes, replacement of video head assemblies, for office telephone service, expenditures for travel, entertainment and association dues. There are also the subscriptions to papers, periodicals and books pertinent to the operation of the department and, of course, the light, heat, and water at studio and transmitter buildings.

Salaries are a major item under product costs. The salary expenditure will be determined by such factors as: the number of studios run simultaneously; the total number of hours per day that are programmed to the air; vacation pay and amount of vacation relief required; holiday pay; night-turn differential, or short turn-around where applicable; overtime and/or replacement personnel to cover illness and/or remote activity.

It may be seen from the above that the Engineering Department is, in a sense, its own purchasing agent. Expenditure requests for major equipment are usually submitted for approval to top management a few months prior to the next calendar year. Similarly, budgets are projected in advance. Both the annual facilities request and the operating budgets of all departments are determined in a joint meeting with all department heads and the general manager.

THE ROLE OF THE ENGINEERING DEPARTMENT

The Engineering Department in a television station is a service function. Its primary objective is—that the equipment will operate without failure; that there will be no switching errors; that there will always be maximum power; that the technicians will conform to the whims of the artists; that an extra man or additional equipment will be found, as if by some magic, for those last minute "brainstorms."

In actuality, the Engineering Department provides the strength and stability, the professional dedication and know-how, which are the very foundation upon which a television station must operate. It could be said, in short, that whereas the Sales Department provides the nourishment and the Program Department the life, the Engineering Department provides the state of being.

The responsibilities of the chief engineer basically encompass the areas of plant, technical equipment, and administration; they require a thorough and continually expanding knowledge of the technical aspects of television. An ability to communicate this knowledge to associates whose talents and skills lie in other realms of endeavor is a further necessity. Nor can the engineer be satisfied with these achievements, for there is still much more he must contribute. He must be sensitive to the programming goals of the station's producers and directors so as to help them realize their aesthetic aspirations in the technical aspects of their programs. Further, the chief engineer must be responsive to the management needs of his company so that he can provide the best possible technical performance within the financial limitations that must be imposed on his, as on all, departments. The chief engineer is also responsible for the administration of his functions and the task of eliciting the best possible technical performance from his own staff. Finally, in a highly technical field he must help the many important non-technical executives and workers realize their goals through the proper use of engineering systems and techniques.

PLANT FACILITIES

While we are primarily considering here the management and operation of the television station as a going concern, a brief review of the planning involved in the construction of a new station will be helpful in understanding the technical requirements of the physical plant.

The location of the transmitter plant is dictated by many factors, such as: cost of land, direction of the city's growth, facilities for parking and public transportation. Local terrain (hills, valleys, flat lands) may require a high tower with high antenna gain which would require less transmitting power; or a directional antenna system to prevent wasted signal over large masses of water or unpopulated areas or to protect another station on the same channel from interference. The radiated transmitter power required will be determined by the total area to be covered (this will be limited, however, by the maximum radiated power allowed by the FCC). Moreover, the location and height of the tower may be subject to possible conflicts with the flight patterns of nearby airports or by local zoning restrictions. These are just a few of the factors that relate to the engineering of a plant long before it goes on the air, all of which will have a direct bearing on the station's subsequent cost of operation.

The size of the transmitter building will be influenced by its proximity to the major metropolitan area which, in turn, will bear on whether or not studio and office personnel will be housed at the transmitter site. Too frequently, the location of the transmitter (so as to enable maximum coverage of the market area) is such that only a small part of the station's other functions can be combined. In any event, consideration must be given to providing emergency power and living facilities for transmitter personnel, as well as standby antennae and transmitting equipment (without which the reliability of the station's transmitting could be seriously affected).

As to studios and offices, space requirements will be dictated by the size of the staff, the number of studios and other operating areas deemed necessary by the management team for the operation of the station. Ample space should be available for expansion in all directions for all activities, including storage for props and field equipment.

Space must be allocated for a technical shop; a general equipment room to include camera, control and miscellaneous rack-mounted equipment; videotape machines and tape storage; film projection equipment; and storage areas for feature film libraries and for commercial or promotional film that will be used.

The physical size of the studios will depend primarily on the amount and scope of live programming. One large studio may suffice, or a second may be needed in order to program live to the air at the same time the other studio is videotaping other programs. The studios should, of course, be designed to accommodate the number of sets or staging areas anticipated; otherwise, restaging or resetting several times a day may become both time-consuming and costly. Lighting requirements, too, are compounded when the same area is used for too many sets.

Each control room should have sufficient flexibility to run the complete program schedule from sign-on to sign-off. This entails the inter-mixture of network, videotape, film and live programming. In addition, it may be desirable to operate two different studios from the same control room. It should be noted, in this connection, that the quality of the on-air show will tend to suffer if too many activities go on simultaneously from a common control room.

TECHNICAL FACILITIES

The video and audio facilities equipment in the studios may be at a minimum in a station that presents primarily film and network programs. Obviously, as the operations expand, the technical requirements become more and more complex. Additional equipment is needed to produce local live programming. The total number of film cameras, film and slide projectors, live camera chains and videotape machines will depend on the programming requirements. Maximum productivity by operating personnel and facilities can be achieved if there is sufficient equipment so that one set is available for on-air use and another is available for producing programs on videotape. Let us now consider the equipment and its use in greater detail.

VIDEO AND AUDIO SWITCHING

Assume that there are four film pick-up cameras and three live studio cameras to intermix. Each one of these seven cameras is fed into a "switcher bus" having seven inputs and one output. A selection of any one of these seven cameras is available in the output of this row of switches. A single switcher such as this (referred to as a 7 x 1 switcher) is used to achieve a direct switch or change of picture from one camera to another. Additional types of switching transitions, such as fades and super-impositions, can be achieved by adding another 7 x 1 switcher with each input common to the first 7 x 1 switcher. The output signals from these two rows of 7 x 1 switchers can then be fed into a mixing amplifier incorporating a dual fader control.

To fade between the two live studio cameras, first the button for one camera is energized on the first 7 x 1 row of switching buttons, then the proper button for the second camera on the second 7 x 1 switcher is depressed. Now, when the fader control handle is moved from one extreme to the other, the output signal from this mixing amplifier shows the picture out of first one camera and then, as this fader control handle is moved to the other end of its range, that first picture fades out and the second picture fades in. When the dual assembly is in the mid position of its range, one picture is super-imposed on the other. The switcher just described is commonly referred to as a 7 x 2 non-composite switcher. It is non-composite in the sense that synchronizing signals will be added at a later point in the over-all system, to effect a complete picture for home receivers.

It is not uncommon for these video switchers to have many more inputs. In the event it is desired to intermix additional live or film camera chains, or to "genlock" to the network and "super" local signals over the network, or to intermix local live film and/or slides over a non-composite videotape signal, more inputs on the non-composite switcher will be needed. Assume, in this instance, that the video switcher has 14 inputs and 5 outputs. The fifth output is called a "direct take bus." This is used as a special "preview bus," to feed key inserts into the special effects equipment. It can also be used for emergency switching inasmuch as it is powered from a source separate from the other switching equipment, thus providing an added factor of reliability in the operation.

In order to key in special effects, "matt" titles over film or studio cameras, to have a special video "wipe" effect, or to set up a split screen picture (that shows half of the picture from one camera and the other half of the picture from the second camera), there must be an additional row of 7 x 2 buttons or switch points stacked upon the first set. Each of the seven buttons must have the same input as is on the first two rows. The output of this second bank of 7 x 2 switch points goes into a special effects mixing amplifier. It has its own dual fader control that changes the special effects type of transition as its fader assembly is moved through its range. Often it is desirable to preset these special effects. Therefore, the output of the mixing amplifier in the first instance, and the output of the special effects amplifier in the second instance, are fed into an additional switching assembly (called a 2 x 1 assembly). The video signal now transmitted in the output of that system will depend on which of the two buttons is selected on this second switcher. The number of inputs of this switcher can be expanded and will vary in accordance with the number of combinations to be achieved.

Just as there must be flexibility in intermixing visual effects from film, live cameras, tape machines, or the network, there must also be flexibility for switching the audio sources from different film projectors, videotape machines, announce booths, audio tape, tape cartridges and/or discs, and often from a number of studio microphones. Therefore, it is evident that the audio console requires a number of input combinations, and should also have two or three output combinations.

As mentioned earlier, there is a video output signal from each control point. This video, along with the output audio from each control point, is fed into a channel switching system. The other inputs into this channel switching system will come from videotape machines, network or remotes.

For example, studio A control point may be originating a program that is being fed to videotape machine #1. At the same time, studio B may be originating a local film program that is being fed to the transmitter. While these functions are going on simultaneously, it may be necessary to record and videotape the signal from the network or feed the network to the clients' room—or still another set of situations may arise. To summarize, in a more complex operation, the channel output switching system could require as many as 10 inputs and 6 outgoing circuits.

CAMERA CHAINS

The technical facilities of television are undergoing rapid and continuing change. This is dramatically apparent in the case of "camera chains." In the early days of television, the iconoscope camera was used primarily for film. This camera is now outdated and has been replaced by the vidicon camera, which offers many technical advantages and better picture quality. The vidicon camera is also being utilized under limited conditions for live studio application, and will undoubtedly find additional usage for this application as improvements are made.

At one time, iconoscope tubes were used in cameras for live studio productions, but these tubes required very high light levels in order to reproduce an acceptable studio picture. Coincident with this light level were the problems of excessive heat and the subsequent stringent air-conditioning requirements. Shortly after the war, however, a camera chain employing the image orthicon tube became commercially available. This tube was extremely sensitive compared to the iconoscope and reproduced highly acceptable picture quality while requiring much less light. As of today, this tube still has wide usage. As a matter of fact, there are several types of 3-inch image orthicon tubes available. Some types are very sensitive for remote work under low light conditions; and others display high resolution with low noise for videotape application; while still others employ a field mesh which improves the gray scale and minimizes halations around picture objects.

Recently, 4½-inch image orthicon tubes have been imported from Europe and have been so widely used that now U.S. companies are manufacturing both the tube and the camera equipment. This tube has several advantages over the 3-inch version, particularly in the area of resolution, signal-to-noise ratio and gray-scale reproduction, all of which contribute to superior pictures. Several manufacturers are now developing a combination of image orthicon and vidicon type tubes in a single camera for use in color, for both live and film programming.

VIDEOTAPE

With the advent of videotape, technical reproduction quality comparable to a live program became possible. Thus, the Program Department may now tape a show in rehearsal, then rerun the tape— to do a critique of the show to determine how it can be improved. Videotape also has permitted taping of three or four live shows at different times and the subsequent playing of them on the air back-to-back. Videotape allows the televising of programs in time periods that otherwise would have required an extra crew or overtime pay for a live production. Further, videotape has been used to expedite national and world-wide news service coverage by eliminating the delays in shipping film across the country. Now, newsfilm is put on a network line, taped at various stations, and aired sometimes within minutes of its receipt.

Equipment is now available for editing tape electronically. This saves cutting tape. Likewise, stop-motion or animated effects can now be produced with accessory equipment that has been developed for videotape machines.

PROJECTION EQUIPMENT

The needs of television have not only stimulated the development of videotape, but have also brought about changes in traditional projection equipment. 16mm and 35mm projectors have been designed specifically for transmitting motion picture film. In some instances standard projectors were revised for this application, and a "continuous motion" picture projector is also available. Most of the stations have 16mm projectors, including other types of slide and opaque projectors. 35mm projectors are used primarily in network operations.

PL Circuits

Programming and engineering people directly involved in producing a show require inter-communications between each position, which in essence amounts to a party line (PL), in order to receive instructions from the program director.

Therefore, there will be a headset at each of the following positions: the program director, technical director, floor men, cameramen, video shaders, audiomen, microphone boom operators, projectionists and videotape operators. This PL should incorporate additional circuits that will permit a cameraman and/or maintenance man to communicate with each other in the event that technical difficulties arise. This will permit them to correct the difficulties without cluttering up the program communications circuit.

Another type of inter-communication that may be required is the "squawk box" or SA system. Controls should be available at the program director's and technical director's operating position, as well as in each of the other operating areas such as projection and videotape. These controls should include a microphone and a speaker at each position, with a control panel that can be energized to call any one of the other positions individually or on a simultaneous basis. An added feature that has been found very advantageous is an over-ride circuit. For example, if the technical director is discussing a problem with the projectionist and a crisis develops at the videotape machine, the videotape operator can over-ride and get the TD's attention, at the same time the TD is in communication with the projectionist. This degree of flexibility has proven highly desirable.

The program director also needs a talk-back circuit to the studio so that he can get the attention of everyone on the floor, and give general instructions to the complete studio crew and talent during rehearsal periods. A similar type of talk-back is equally desirable for the technical director and the audioman from their control positions to the studio.

ADDITIONAL TECHNICAL FACILITIES

We have touched on just a few of the major equipment requirements of a television station. Projection room equipment and videotape machines are major items of equal importance, but the items
covered thus far in themselves do not constitute a complete station
package. We have mentioned that the live and film cameras are
routed to several different points. The same is true of the signals
from the network and videotape machines. Therefore, distribution
amplifiers and a number of other items are also required for telecasting. Such items include:

Sync Generators

Pulse Distribution Amplifiers

Genlock Facilities

Video Distribution Amplifiers

Preview Monitors and Oscilloscopes
  (for network, remote, film cameras, live cameras, tape machines)

On-Air Monitors

Audio Distribution Amplifiers

Power Supplies

Audio Tape and Cartridge Playback
  Machines

Videotape Facilities

16mm Sound-on-Film Projectors
  with Magnetic Sound Attachment

2 x 2 Slide Projectors (other sizes
  may be required)

Projectors for Opaque Material

Multiplexers
  (to intermix film and slide projectors into film camera chains)

Rear Screen Projectors
  (for slide and/or film in live studio productions)

Live Studio Camera Chains, Film
  Camera Chains

Microphones

Radio Microphones

Microphone Booms, Live Camera
  Pedestals

Studio Lighting Fixtures
  (for over-all illumination, including backlight and special effects
  light pattern projectors)

Studio Light Dimmer Board
  (with patch panel, two scene preset and master faders for fast
  change of lighting sequences)

Auxiliary Studio Light Pockets

Test Equipment
  (including various types of special oscilloscopes, frequency and
  distortion measurement equipment for audio and video, tools,
  and other items too numerous to
  mention)

FACILITIES FOR REMOTES

A number of stations require a mobile video unit housing basic
equipment to generate from a remote location television programs
such as baseball or football games, banquets, speeches, and many
other special events. The equipment required will include most of

the facilities, except for film projectors already discussed, as part of the normal station facilities. What is unusual, of course, is that such equipment should be packaged for portable use.

A mobile videotape machine may be desirable at the remote location; or the signal from the remote can be fed to the studio via leased video and audio lines; or via a microwave transmitter link beaming the signal from the remote back to the studio so that this signal can go directly on the air; or be recorded on a videotape machine at the studio.

The cost of video circuits from a remote can be a major item if temporary towers have to be constructed to provide line-of-sight for the microwave equipment. In some instances, there will not be a line-of-sight path from the remote location to the receiver of the microwave link at the studio, then two or three or more of these units may be required to provide a multi-hop link. Often times it may be necessary to provide emergency power equipment to run the mobile units.

TECHNICAL FACILITIES IN OTHER DEPARTMENTS

Stations actively engaged in news and public affairs programming usually require assistance from the Engineering Department in selecting the type of cameras for slides as well as sound-on-film work, and various type lenses required for such activity.

Quite frequently, too, a local film laboratory is not available during the hours that newsfilm has to be processed. In some instances, therefore, it has proven more economical to provide film processing equipment. Additional equipment required for previewing, editing and splicing the film will also have to be acquired.

The News Department may have several mobile vehicles with two-way radio equipment. These will require FCC licenses as well as installation and subsequent maintenance. Normally, the base station for this activity is located at the studio. Its control point is in the News Department, but licensing and maintenance are responsibilities of the Engineering Department.

The development of transistorized solid state devices permitting miniaturization of cameras and videotape machines will have a major impact on the current methods of gathering news material.

The Film Department is responsible for the preparation of

feature film as well as the integration of commercials, promotion and public service announcements for air use. This activity requires film projectors for viewing, footage counters and editing equipment. Again, the Engineering Department assists in the recommendation of suitable types of equipment, its purchase and subsequent maintenance.

Most of the offices in a television station may be equipped with either a special line drive video and audio monitor or with standard television receivers, connected to a master antenna distribution system. This system will not only permit selection of all the local channels in a city, but will also make it possible to incorporate, for closed circuit use, one of the unassigned channels in the city by means of a local RF generator that can be fed video and audio signals from the tape machines, from a studio rehearsal, or for a film or network screening that can be seen by other station personnel in their respective offices.

TECHNICAL CHALLENGES

The television broadcast industry is still growing rapidly. The creation of programming that is new and exciting is a continuous goal. The changes and the advancements place ever more stringent requirements on engineering personnel and equipment. The technician must become more of a "programmeer" than ever before. He must be able to contribute to the creative and aesthetic goals of the program director in order that the end product be as professional as possible. Fortunately, a number of technical personnel have been able to bridge this gap. The technician can no longer afford to be just a "button pusher"—even though he is still expected to push the right button at the right time. There have been great strides in the technological advancement of equipment and it is the technician's responsibility to keep abreast of the changes as his plant is updated.

New approaches to equipment design are sorely needed. For example, the current method of handling film spots such as commercials, promotional and/or public announcements is very laborious and time consuming. Audio tape cartridges solved a similar problem for radio, by replacing the ET's. An automatic film cartridge for TV is sorely needed as is a videotape cartridge. Similarly, each station displays a large number of slides in its day-to-day operation and each one must be loaded individually. There are some types of slide projectors on the market that hold up to 100 slides in each chamber, but we are in need of a hopper arrangement whereby the slides can be stacked (not loaded) in consecutive order, one on top of the other, so that they can be shown without interruption.

Programming needs are becoming more complex day by day. Some stations have turned to automation as a means of coping with the problem; and this is a quite feasible solution for many hours during the broadcast day, with the possible exception of live studio productions. In fact, a more sophisticated approach to automation of a station's schedule from the inception of a sales and/or program order, through the various departments, could provide significant progress. These are just a few of the areas that need attention. The opportunities for people and equipment in broadcasting are constantly expanding.

Index

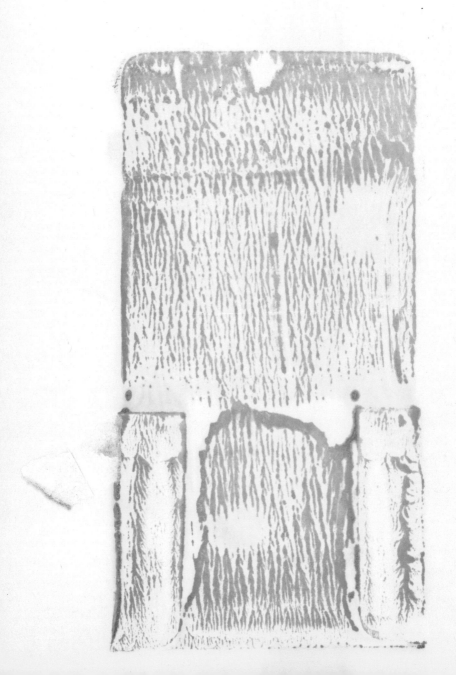